TREVOR'S STORY

Trevor Jones

Canadian Cataloguing in Publication Data

Jones, Trevor Lloyd, 1909-
 Trevor's story

 ISBN 1-55212-288-3

 1. Jones, Trevor Lloyd, 1909- 2. Veterinarians—Canada
—Biography. 1. Title.
SF613.J66A3 1999 636.089'092   C99-911093-4

TRAFFORD

This book was published *on-demand* in cooperation with Trafford Publishing.
On-demand publishing is a unique process and service of making a book available for retail sale to the public taking advantage of on-demand manufacturing and Internet marketing.
On-demand publishing includes promotions, retail sales, manufacturing, order fulfilment, accounting and collecting royalties on behalf of the author.

Suite 2, 3050 Nanaimo St., Victoria, B.C. V8T 4Z1, CANADA
Phone   250-383-6864   Toll-free   1-888-232-4444 (Canada & US)
Fax   250-383-6804   E-mail   sales@trafford.com
Web site   www.trafford.com   TRAFFORD PUBLISHING IS A DIVISION OF TRAFFORD HOLDINGS LTD.
Trafford Catalogue #99-0039   www.trafford.com/robots/99-0039.html

10   9   8   7   6   5   4   3   2

SALEM

A distinctive Welsh symbol

CONTENTS

INTRODUCTION

*In my old age I have accepted Voltaire's solution
to his hero, Candide, by finding happiness in my
garden, although my garden has now been reduced
to a well kept patio, and that suits me fine at 90.*

Some of my friends will have read my use of the above in a different context. But then, as we shall see, quite a bit of what will follow has already been in print sometime in my life.

One's 90th birthday can be a memorable occasion. Mine was. My wife Marjorie had prepared a display of pictures, covering three 40" x 28" old frames. They were crowded with family photos, from my babyhood to the time I became an old man.

Many of the 54 guests at Marjorie's party commented to me some modification of the phrase, "You must write it down Trevor!", and one asked about my earliest recollection. That was easy. Two years and thirty four days after my birth day I was given a large cup to celebrate the coronation of King George V and Queen Mary. The date was on the cup, June 22, 1911.

For four months after the party I had been heeding my friends' suggestion. I have been writing it down for my own enjoyment. Suffused with memories of a busy life and with articles I have written from time to time, including descriptions of events and places I have visited as a consultant in international development - all of this I have cobbled together to coax myself into a hobby for my retirement. But I have been persuaded that I have a story to share. It cannot be said that I started this too soon; I did not leap before I looked! By starting at 90, however, I had little time to dawdle, not knowing how much time I had left, but with no thought of publishing my first book.

It has been said that all Welsh people are manic depressives. Would this be because we are a vanquished race? I was born of Welsh parents and lived in Wales for my first 20 years, before coming to Canada. That was a period of joy for me. It was sprinkled with love and pride over a culture that emphasized a distinctive language, literature and harmony in music but hardly allows for a racewide mental weakness.

When jobs were scarce, during the economic depression of the 20s, an uncle kept me occupied on his farm in Wales. He was a diabetic and I supplied the physical labour to replace the strength he had lost. It turned out that this was just what I needed to focus on the things of real worth. I was working hard, eating and sleeping well in contrast with the doldrums I had gone through after leaving school.

Shortly after settling into my adopted country I had a letter from my mother's brother, Llewelyn, which ended, "I understand you don't have to be ashamed of being a Welshman in Canada". This gave me pause to admit that the occasional sign of an inferiority complex is shown in my country of origin. No pity and, never in Canada! However, the compelling exercise in writing that I've just been through has heightened my emotional temperature, while dwelling on the reveries of my childhood. There is little I want to forget of those years.

In a treasurehouse of memories some fail to surface at the time they would be in context. My aged mind is the excuse I give for that. During the time I was Dean of the Ontario Veterinary College there were problems with controversy arising. This goes along with the job, but my treasurehouse has not permitted these to survive.

ACKNOWLEDGEMENTS

My wife's constant encouragement and kindness in reading proofs and her gracious readiness to be cheerful at all times was appreciated throughout. I thank my neighbour, Jeanne Keech, who has put my almost illegible manuscript on the computer and has supplied me with proofed copy. Heather Logan assisted particularly with Appendix Two. Jean McDonald, David Bain and Dr. R.P. Briggs gave helpful advice from time to time.

The Walker Art Gallery has given permission to include a copy of *Salem*. Use of the caricature on the cover was approved by the University of Toronto Press but I have been unable to contact relatives of the late Paul Buchanan. He drew the pen sketch for a "Century of Challenge" in 1962.

1
BEING NINETY

I am a survivor. I have survived two world wars and a period of serious economic depression in the normal period for carving out a career. As I write this, I am ninety years old. I'm in the process of putting scraps of manuscript together for my own enjoyment and I find there is a story to be told.

One can close one's eyes to reality but not to memories. They pop up, especially after a refreshing sleep. Early yesterday morning I found myself thinking about my earliest memories. I recall pointing to the flat tray of unbroken taffy, and saying to the lady behind the counter, "I'll have a penny-worth of this one," whereupon I gave her a furtive glance and pressed hard on the nearby broken taffy tray, with the sleeve of my jersey, and doubled my take. No, this couldn't be my earliest memory because it happened when I knew right from wrong and I was enjoying being naughty! But, still in the mood to find my earliest memory, I got out of bed to get confirmation about the date, June 22, 1911, which appeared on a mug celebrating the coronation of King George V and Queen Mary. What was the significance of that date for me, just two years and 34 days after my birth? Early in the morning my sister Gwen gave me a bath in the tub before the kitchen fire. She loved to mother me and I learned early to submit

We were to be at the Church of England School at 9 o'clock. After breakfast I was put in the go-cart. This travelled on four wheels, a sort of chair, with carpet material from the handles to the front of the seat. Remember them? Gwen pushed me to the school, arriving at about 8.45, and I was presented with this Coronation tot with the picture of the Royal couple and the date. I was the baby of a family of five but it escapes me why this qualified me to be the recipient of such a prize.

My mother had five children in six years. Jim was the eldest, then Arthur, Gwen, Olwen and me. We had a happy childhood; the front room

Trevor at eighteen months.

Five children in six years; from right: Jim, Arthur, Gwen, Olwen and Trevor.

became the playroom in a house too small for eight people, including Laura the maid.

When it came time for James to start piano lessons my father became concerned about the German upright piano. It was in the playroom so he had it encased with wood panels in front, to be removed for practice time by turning wing nuts beyond our reach. They were no barrier for Arthur; he was *mwddrwg* (a devil) and by using chairs and our help he climbed over the top.

In passing, by writing *mwddrwg* I am reminded of the many words in Welsh requiring no vowel! For example, there is *grwng* for grunt, *mwswgl* for moss, *gwrdd* for vehement, *mwlwch* for sweepings, and so on.

But I digress. In time, Jim played the harmonium in chapel. The girls in turn took to the piano but not very well, and Arthur and I never got very far beyond scratching on the violin.

On Sunday afternoons at four my father paraded us in front of the grandfather clock to hear the verse we had learned for reciting at the evening chapel service. Capel Bethel was the social centre in my childhood. It was of the protestant, non-conformist persuasion known as

Anibynwyr Cynulleidfaol - Independent Congregationalist. This was the first of the nonconformist breakaway from the Church of England, following the reformation of Henry VIII. We were the protesting protestants that descended from Oliver Cromwell's Independents.

We did not express the emotionalism of the Fundamentalists but were in the Puritan tradition, with no ritual. What emotion we showed stemmed from the notion that Welsh was the language of heaven and that the Welsh harp would have pride of place there!

Capel Bethel - organ in memory of Trevor's father and uncle.

7

Trevor's mother as a young lady.

Although Welsh was our first language and we spoke it at home, it was soon lost after we started school, where the language of instruction throughout our schooling was English. When alone, my parents spoke Welsh but eventually the influence of school dominated and, with the exception of Arthur, the rest of us ceased to be bilingual. A prime qualification for Arthur when he became a bank manager was his ability to speak Welsh.

We ended up understanding more than we could speak but if salvation surfaced in chapel it escaped us. We were disciplined in the best possible way through love for our parents and there never was a hint of rebellion in attending chapel three times a Sunday. Services were always in Welsh and the whole congregation sang hymns lustily, often improvising into a six part harmony and repeating the last two lines once or twice through a reluctance to give up the *hwyl* (emotional ambience).

After evening service, the children stayed behind to learn new hymn tunes. By Spring, congregations of a like persuasion in our part of the country would convene at Capel Bethel for a festival of hymn singing - *Gymanfa ganu.* So, we hatched a new batch of hymn tunes each year. No wonder I didn't know any of the hymns after an absence of 2 years overseas. The *Gymanfa ganu* ended up with the Hallelujah Chorus, and what a rousing finality there was to that!

When we were in sunday school on Sunday afternoons my father would have a well earned rest in bed. He was 53 when I was born and in the context of the day, I knew him only as an old man. He spoke very little about his early life and, by the time I was old enough to observe, he had settled into a routine. His day started with breakfast in bed, followed by a period of socializing with my mother, who would stand at the foot of the four poster and they would chat pleasantly until dad was ready to get up. This was the only chance for a quiet time together.

First thing, he would fill his pipe with *Amlwch Shag* then go to the bathroom. When he came out clouds of permeating pipe smoke came with him. Here's an anachronism which he wouldn't have knowledge of: he always wore a jacket long out of style known as a cut-away, and he always wore starched collars.

By now it was about 10 o'clock and he would leave for his place of business. To get there he would walk through "The Private". This was a private road which led to our large vegetable gardens and small apple orchard. To avoid the Private from becoming public dad would lock it now and again. This was always a challenge to me and my friends. The high wall was topped with clinkers and broken glass, mortared into them. On the climb over at least one of us was bound to draw blood.

I am reminded of another feature along the Private. There was a high wall enclosing the yard behind the Royal Oak Pub. There was a notice at the front of the pub, "Stallion at Stud Wednesday mornings." I was just a nipper but I climbed the high wall to check this entertainment. This was my first encounter with procreation. I was immature enough at the time for the thought to arise - surely mam and dad didn't do that, in spite of the information coming from the bigger boys at school.

My father and his brother Robert were seed merchants. They had inherited the business from their step-father under the name of Davies and Sons, Victoria House. They also sold animal feed and a bakery. While most of the business took place in a large warehouse, the front, on the High Street, was a grocer's shop.

Their busiest time was in the early spring. Uncle Robert would visit the farmers to help them decide on the seed mixtures for pastures and what was called corn, which meant anything but corn as we know it. A corn crop in Britain refers to wheat, oats and barley.

Dad kept informed with the Manchester Dispatch and the Liverpool Echo each day, and for local news, the monthly County Herald, from Flint. The world of these two mild, loveable brothers seems very small and uncomplicated but they were happy in each other's company. They would smoke their last pipe on lighting up at their office around 9 o'clock, one to the uproar of five young children and the other to Aunty Katie, who kept the five of us under control as well as her daughter Gwyneth. They walked the Private with their pipes gleaming as they breathed in the cold, damp air through well used pipe stems.

The emotion arising from favourite hymn tunes remained untouched as I grew up. One of these is the well known tune "Jerusalem". When I visited the Holy City half a century after leaving Bethel I felt an emotional experience, but the place of the hymn tune was in an entirely separate category of my memory.

When I was 9, I composed a hymn which my mother sent to the editor of *Tywysydd Y Plant* - Children's Leader. I saw my name in print for the first time.

Hymn of Love

O my loving Jesus	I would not choose my way.
Guard me lest I stray	But Thou hast chosen me
Lead me with Thine own hand	To be Thy faithful worker
Every night and day.	To all Eternity.
When shall come the Peace time	We are like the ocean,
As in the realms above,	Rolling far away
Where no evil dwelleth	But with Thy love, O Jesus!
But good and perfect love?	We shall never stray.

The editor announced a competition for his readers under the age of 16 to translate. Many in the hinterland there would be to do this.

Losing our language was the most serious impediment to retaining our cultural inheritance. We were only eleven miles from Chester, with its fullness of England's history. Capel Bethel was our main link with our Welshness, so that language and religion seemed synonymous. It became easy for us to regard Welsh as the language of heaven, while anything English tended to belong to Mammon. Love of our native land, its language, customs and culture, held their place for us as we grew up but even as children we recognized the compulsion which said, you better have knowledge of English if you want to get on. This helped us to discover that life is a window, not a mirror reflecting only ourselves. Life is a window with an unending panorama that invites the willing ones to "put the pipe to powerful lips". But for us it did not require the vanquished to abandon their roots.

It is easy to overdo the biblical admonition, "Ye cannot serve God and Mammon" and many a Welshman colours the truth in the pub on week nights, while "speaking it plain" in chapel on Sunday. You get the drift? Sunday is for God, week days for Mammon, and the boss is so often English.

I liken this attitude to the situation in Quebec before the quiet revolution. The main difference here is the link with Rome was being unleashed, while with us, as a vanquished nation, we clutched our Welsh bible with both hands as a symbol to the victors - "Oh ye of little faith".

Obviously, I am remembering experiences of my youth with no reference to the changes that evolved. Remarkable changes have occurred, particularly since the end of the second world war. Relations with Westminster have improved and in the bid in May 1999 to obtain more political autonomy Alan Michael, the labour leader, who was two votes short of a majority, has been nominated the first leader in the new Assembly. Lord Dafydd Elis-Thomas, leader of the National Party, was made Speaker. Michael intends to persuade the rival parties to support Labour's policies, on a case by case basis. The Welsh dragon is finding compromise far more suitable than the turbulence that characterized his ancient past.

The Red Dragon (*Ddraig Goch*) was the central feature of the Welsh National Flag which became authorised in 1958, but it has been a symbol of welshness since time immemorial.

It has breathed fire to stir the spirits of the people throughout the ages.

In the first decade and a half of the 15th century, the chief hero of the people, Owain Glyn Dwr unfurled a dragon banner in victory and defeat, as the emblem of the spirit of independence of the Welsh nation.

Chosen as the mascot for the Rugby World Cup competition in 1999, the Welsh dragon welcomed visitors who came to that event from all world regions.

Like the Celts who were the progenitors of my race, I embrace this symbol in my dawning and in my dew.

A nephew, Prof. Ian Fleming of Cambridge University travelled the farthest to be at Trevor's 90th birthday on March 19, 1999.

2
MOLD

Mold, a town in North Wales, had a population of about 4000 when I was born there in 1909. My education began early. I was in the infants class at the Church of England School when I was three. This proved to be more of a babysitting service than the beginning of my formal education, but not a very successful one at that. Gwen would take me home at noon with a tale more than once: "Mam, Trevor's wet his pants again."

I have few happy recollections of my school days. In the winter for instance, sitting about eight rows from the fireplace. This has remained as a discomforting memory and a serious handicap at the time I was learning to write. I could not control my fingers. The teacher would allow each row of pupils to stand close to the fire for about 10 minutes during a lesson period, but this was a mere gesture.

Mold, High Street.

Mold Church of England School, 1920 soccer team. Trevor as manager is next but one from the Vicar.

The popular headmaster of my day, J.R. Macfarlane, used me to carry messages around the school, to offices and other places in town. He also made me manager of the football team (see photo). I became complaisant and at the same time complacent; not worrying enough about completing my homework. In high school there was a handicap, over the fact that the Headmaster, William Lloyd Parry, was my father's cousin. We were to seek no favours but the family was to show exemplary scholarship and behaviour. I found it difficult to shine in either. Like the girl who can't dance, says the band can't play, I was apt to complain that I had poor teachers.

Mr. Shaw, the sports master, was well liked by everyone, including me. One day he called me aside: "Jones, you are not following the family tradition. Both of your brothers in their day were valuable members of the soccer and cricket teams. You are on neither and I notice you have not put down for participation on sports day. I insist that you enter at least one event." I chose the hundred yards dash, and came in last!

On looking back, I don't understand why I did not try for the soccer team because nearly all my free time was spent playing soccer with a large circle of friends. Did it cease to be a competitive sport in those circumstances, I wonder?

To be fair, I had good teachers and some who were not inspiring. Miss Wilson was the Headmistress and the weight of her own ego made it difficult to like her. Her method of teaching history left me numb about the subject. Every lesson began with, "Pencils and tablets quickly," followed by a rush to transfer her words onto our tablets without any notion that once upon a time there were facts of flesh, blood and dynamism.

Mr. Higgins, who succeeded Miss Wilson as my history teacher, was a delightful contrast. He made the pupils feel like participants. Sometimes he would give assignments with the expectation of being called on at the next lesson. Once he said to me: "Jones, I give you one word, 'Bosworth'. Give the class a brief account of your reading at the lesson on Thursday."

I began nervously as I recall but from memory my comments went something like this:

> At Bosworth Field, Sir, in 1485 the House of Tudor replaced the House of Lancaster as the reigning sovereign of the British throne. King Richard III, in spite of having a superiority of more than 7000 men and by far a more commanding position, was killed in battle and the cry went up, 'King Harry', as Richard's crown was placed on the head of Henry Tudor, on the battle field. Henry Tudor, Earl of Richmond was proclaimed King Henry VII and the Tudors reigned from 1485 to the death of Queen Elizabeth I in 1603. The Battle of Bosworth Field had the effect of ending the Wars of the Roses and the Hundred Years War in Europe. It is said that Henry VII was not a particularly nice person but he wasn't as wily as his successor, Henry VIII.
> At this stage sir, my father looked over my shoulder, checking my homework. "You are right," he said, "the aristocrats in Wales did well by the Tudors but both the Henrys continued to suppress the use of our language. Regulations forbade welsh to be spoken in court, in school, and even in the school yard."
> The Tudors brought peace and prosperity for 22 years but the expectation that Wales would be more generously dealt with at Westminster did not materialize. It was my father's view that apart from the gentry, the average welshman felt no advantage to him following the Battle of Bosworth Field.

Let me admit that I became a disciple of Mr. Higgins but none of the others came close.

By the time I was 17 both of my parents had died. Memories of my father on his deathbed remind me of the good fortune I had growing up in a family with great love and respect for our parents. My mother died when I was eleven and the housekeeper, as much as she tried, did not fill the gap. My grieving period seemed a long one, with little help to assuage my loss.

As I think of my father shortly before he died, my guilty conscience insists that I record the following: "Dad, I'm the only one without a gold watch to remember you by." His voice was weak but not resentful. "Tell Mr. Saum, the jeweller, I sent you to choose a gold watch as a remembrance gift."

My father died in 1926. Two years before he died, he took me for an interview with his bank manager. He wanted me to continue in the same career as my older brothers. I believe the main reason for this chosen pattern was his seeming obsession about security and a reasonable guarantee of lifetime employment. As it turned out, my father's last illness meant that no further step was taken with the bank manager beyond the first interview.

One of my childhood delights was to visit my grandparents home, *Maesgarmon Farm*, just 2 miles outside Mold. In the big kitchen there hung a large print of Curnow Vosper's masterpiece *Salem* (see Frontispiece). This picture has endeared itself to the Welsh family home. It hung where all could see it, as a symbol of Welshness and a statement about our distinctive nationality.

In his book, written in Welsh, Tal Williams, the author of *Salem* (*Cyhoethiadau Barthas,* 1991) has given us a detailed account of each character in Vosper's picture and many other details. Happily, the book has been translated into English so that a lapsed Welsh speaker like me can enjoy it. A close look at the picture will reveal the subtle outline of the head of the devil in the folds of the shawl of Sian Owen, the principal character. One wag has it that Salem is a caricature of Welsh piety and hypocracy!

My mother grew up on this farm of about 500 acres. My grandparents had ten children. One died in infancy, with five boys and four girls remaining. *Maesgarmon* was one of the most productive farms in the neighborhood. Grandfather was fortunate to have five ablebodied sons as a captive group and they all learned the skills of farming at home before venturing on their own.

When Llewelyn, the eldest son, got married, *Nain* (grandmother) gave him a horse named *Blod* as a wedding present and uncle drove it about 25 miles to *Ffordd Criccen*, near Rhuddlan, where he began farming for himself. But *Blod* would have none of it. She escaped from the pasture and retraced her steps!

Maesgarmon family, Trevor's mother, bottom left.

The four sisers of the *Maesgarmon* family participated in the production of dairy products - they all made butter and cheese. My mother was sent to a dairy institute to learn about making the different kinds of cheeses. In her day there were a mere 2 or 3 compared to the numerous kinds developed during my generation. She delayed her suitor's offer of marriage because this required her to live with her prospective mother-in-law! As soon as the shop was closed on a Friday night, dad would tuck the County Herald under his waistcoat to keep the damp cold air out, and walk over two miles to meet his lady love. He was 46 when confetti was thrown at their wedding and mam was 34. By that time 3 of the 4 sisters were married to unrelated men named Jones.

When I was 6 years old I had a number of health problems. A tubercular lymph gland was removed from my neck, I had my tonsils and adenoids taken out and in that same year measles showed up for the second time. The languid weakness I felt during most of that year is a vivid memory for me today. But the comfort and love that attended mam's nursing remains with me too.

She was a good mother and dad insisted on a live-in maid and a washer woman every Tuesday so that she could devote her time to raising the five children. The house was made emaculate for Sunday so we lived in the cellar on Saturdays with the cleaning being extended to whitening the stone steps at the front door and the one below the gate at the bottom of the garden.

During the first war she knitted a pair of socks for the troops every week and at one stage she wrote to Lloyd George, the P.M., thanking him for his leadership but pleading with him to press for an end to the slaughter.

When the two of us were home alone I would ask mam to talk of her early days in *Maesgarmon* and she told me about a significant historical episode that occurred long long ago. There is a memorial obelisk in one of the fields, known as the Hallelujah Monument. Erected in 1736, it celebrated a victory in AD 420 against the heathen Picts and Saxons. The Latin inscription tells of a battle between the heathen invaders and the local people who fought under the leadership of Saint Germanus. They were hopelessly outnumbered by the enemy. Germanus decided on an unusual strategy. When his priests and followers rose to face the enemy they gave a howling cry of Hallelujah which echoed and re-echoed, whereupon the Picts and Saxons fled in alarm.

One of my grandfather's labourers stuttered rather badly. It happened that the Squire, the landlord of *Maesgarmon*, had a similar impediment. The Squire was walking in a pasture when he came across the labourer and asked him the time. With long stuttering conjunctions, this took a little while. When the labourer offered his reply in the same way, the Squire naturally took offence through ignorance of his problem and molested him with his officer's baton.

Well, my grandfather tried to mollify the offended one and promised to clarify the situation. Always a very fair landlord, Col. Philips was apologetic and handed my grandfather a guinea and said, "G…g…give him this." This pleased the labourer. "Tell the Squire I'll kiss his bottom any time for a guinea."

The cultural life of Wales is nurtured in many ways, and particularly in the several denominations of chapels in every community where the language is still spoken. The word chapel is used to distinguish non-conformist congregations and the Anglican state church.

Children learn harmony and indeed find out they can sing, by the opportunity afforded in chapel. I believe the epigram, Land of Song, stems largely from the early beginning, when a child becomes conscious of having a voice. If you don't sing, you don't know if you have a singing voice!

Another important nurturing institution is the *Eisteddfod*, which perhaps is best described as an assembly of poets and musicians. The record shows that one was held in Camarthen as early as 1430, in Caerwys in 1523 and again in 1568. Nowadays, there are two of them annually, the National *Eisteddfod* which alternates from North to South, and the International, which is permanently placed in Llangollen, in North Wales. The National *Eisteddfod* for 1991 took place at *Maesgarmon*.

A temporary theatre is erected for this purpose, and musicians, choirs, poets, come from all world regions to compete. Highlight of the concert is the crowning of the Bard, an ancient Druidic custom with ceremony around the *Gorsedd* circle of stone pillars outdoors, built for the occasion.

I was 14 when the previous one in Mold took place in 1923. With some of my contemporaries, I felt important, selling programs. The *Eisteddfod* site was a field close to my home. The huge canvas tent had a stage big enough for visiting choirs of 150 voices. Clutching my programs, I shook the hand of Lloyd George as he mounted the stage to wow the audience with his vintage rhetoric.

This was a time on our part for risky episodes of fun and games. David, my friend who later became my brother-in-law, implicated me in an ingenious but naughty set-up. It happened, without the environmentalists of the day objecting, that sanitary arrangements of a temporary nature rested on the banks of a little stream. They were a temptation for David. He got pieces of cork, on which he secured candles. The idea was that we would light the candles, allowing them to float downstream. We observed the outcome when seats were occupied. The resulting chaos was well worthwhile!

This was a time for new social interaction. I paid more attention to girls. There were visitors from South Wales, which seemed almost a foreign country. Blodwen Prytherch in my memory stood out. We found secret places where she taught me new ways to kiss and I mistook lust for love. She seemed to be on a high plane of sophistication compared with the schoolgirls in Mold. But our puppy-love evaporated on exchanging letters and in about six weeks she went out of my life with no feeling of emptiness.

Real emptiness comes with the loss of one's mother. My mother died when she was 52. She had suffered for some years with diabetes before life-giving insulin had been discovered.

My father came to bed and whispered, "Mam has gone." It was the end of the world for me. The intervals between feelings of grief lengthened as they should, over time. But, a visit to Bethel, or memories of loving care during sickness when I was six, the tailored grey serge costume, or the wartime letter she wrote to Lloyd George - all of these and more hover at the edge of my awareness because she died when I was eleven.

Getting used to a housekeeper started a new chapter in my life; "You won't go to bed at night, you can't get up in the morning." Poor Mrs. Edwards was a simple creature but she did her best. To warm her bed in the attic, she would clutch the flat, warm metal shelf from the cast iron oven, wrapped in newspaper. She'd pass through with no authority to make us go to bed.

This was a time of adjustment for all of us. My brothers had friends in for poker, or they went to the cinema or dances and I was caught up in this adults' world while still going to school. Solace for my father was found in his smoke-laden office with his brother. Staying late into the night, Dad's footsteps had us scrambling to make the house scene appear normal.

School had little interest for me. I well remember the character who ran a taxi in Mold. He spent most of his time snoozing in the back seat of his model T Ford, waiting for a fare off the next train at the station. What a fortunate soul, I thought, being paid to drive a car, without really having to work for a living! This was closer to reality than sitting in a classroom.

We children were apprehensive in moving to the secondary level at the Alun County School. As mentioned earlier, the headmaster was my father's cousin, and we were expected to show exemplary discipline in class and in sports. He was deformed and gave the appearance of having a shortened neck. He was a court magistrate. This and the intellect he possessed made him a prominent character and among the elite in the community. He put me in mind of the line from Oliver Goldsmith:

> "And still they gazed, and still the wonder grew
> That one small head could carry all he knew".

Looking back on my school days I can only assume that the model T Ford and the easygoing taxi driver gave me happier thoughts than lessons at hand. As for homework I would think of any excuse for not doing assigned work. My friend Llewelyn Davies was good at Latin and he took it as a tribute that I would use his translations.

Whether I was indifferent through boredom or laziness, I recently came across the description of a syndrome, reminding me of my attitude during those school day experiences. Those who show the symptoms described are said to shed them as they grow up. One of my difficulties was with numbers but I made highest marks in geometry which I found logical. Most subjects were distant from reality and lacked the attraction of driving a model T. I thrived on English composition and have always found a fascination in words. Part of this I think came from learning English as a second language, with the need to spend endless time on vocabulary.

When I was in Form II I found myself attracted to Dol Farr, and it was reciprocated. She was always at the top of the form, or close to it. I think her mother thought it was time to observe Dorothy's handling of passion. The abbreviation pash. was always how Dol and her girl friends would refer to what some of their number had for certain male teachers. Mrs. Farr promoted ours!

Friday evenings were set aside as free from study and I was expected to call at eight. Mrs. Farr would call upstairs, "Nancy, its 8 o'clock" whereupon Dol's older sister and her affianced would leave the fireside of the sitting room and walk the streets. It was our turn.

We knew more about sex than we had experience with it. We'd kiss once in a while but felt no hint of romance. It was beginning but I didn't realise how sensible Mrs. Farr was. Did she know that we were too young to be aroused to our body's mischiefs? I can't remember how long we enjoyed each other's company but we probably separated because I could not match Dol's devotion to schoolwork.

Without inviting psycho analysis I'll add a postscript; Dorothy Farr pursued a career as Warden of one of England's largest prisons.

School days are a time of commitments broken. I soon proceeded with an experimental romance with a close friend of Dol Farr, and this seemed satisfactory to the affected parties. I fell in love with Aelwyn. She had an older sister so I labelled her *eil oen* (second lamb), becoming Wyn for short.

We wished to be in each other's company as much as possible; a sure sign of the burgeoning love. In between we would practise the art of writing love letters.

Sanctioned by her mother, Wyn invited me to *Ty Gwyn* for the weekend. Her father was off to Antwerp on an extra-marital affair. Without comment, her mother evidently knew we would exercise our will to combat the urgent desires of the flesh. We were intimate enough to be in bed together. The free society of today renders it old fashioned to hold on to one's virginity before confetti has been thrown. We retained ours.

This avocation, this glorious romance was shared through Aelwyn's university years, and a period of graduate study in France. But tragedy came when Aelwyn suffered the fulminating type of tuberculosis and died June 20, 1934. By that time I had lived in Canada for five years.

The period between the wars (1918-1939) was my time for growing up and settling into a career. But it was also a time of economic depression. There were no jobs. By every economic yardstick these years caused desperation and hardship, particularly for the hordes of the unemployed. The economy in Wales was particularly hard hit, for example, because of the international competition in coal production, coal being by far the most important item of trade. And the period of depression was extended when the Royal Navy, which was the coal miners' best customer, changed to oil as a source of energy for its ships.

To improve my applications for jobs, I took a course at the Business Training College in Chester. Being a daily train commuter was an exciting change from languishing in Mold! This proved to be a valuable interlude for about two years when, with little else to do, I decided to enrol in agricultural education at the Llysfasi Farm Institute, between Ruthin and Llangollen, near the beautiful Horseshoe Pass in North Wales. This was a happy experience. The course content built on chemistry in high school and the mathematics taught at Chester. But my main memory of Llysfasi was the discomfort of topping and tailing turnips with frost on them and sorting potatoes for size, on cold mornings. I also remember the incessant return day after day of banking - but not the kind my father had in mind. By the vagaries of weather and the action of livestock the banks between fields become eroded. Healing the eroded areas was a constant occupation for youths who chose to learn farming! We would eat a good breakfast then like inmates in a prison we'd form a gang with a shovel over our shoulder to the day's area for bank renewal. This was achieved by transferring sod from the field to fill the gaps in the bank. Well, this was a very pleasant occupation for youths, all under 20, in the prime of good health. The banter betrayed a preoccupation with love and lust but was never vehement. Each of us had discovered our own sexuality, but none, I think, had known a woman - in a biblical sense!

Our custodian was a model of a Welsh country character and of the tenacity of the peasant mind. He had his share of paperwork to keep track of our attendance and performance on the job. Writing is an unfamiliar task for a countryman, not because he can't write but because there has been very little need for this. We used to watch him taking hold of a pencil as

Mold

though it was an axe or a spade. When he became more familiar with his gang his conscience would allow him to ask one of us to be the scribe, but he never allowed us to embroider his remarks.

One incident that comes to mind is the time the Principal, Mr. Isaac Jones, arranged for a bus to spend a day observing some of the programs at the Faculty of Agriculture, University of Wales, Bangor. I was at the back of the bus, he at the front. My classmates' jovial mood prompted me to blurt out:

> Who's the man with the big red nose? (everybody) Who, ha, who ha ha
> The more he drinks the redder it grows, (everybody) Who, ha, who ha ha.

This had a surprising consequence. As Principal Isaac Jones was thanking the Dean of Agriculture for our pleasant day, he concluded: "And I'll now ask one of my students, Mr. Jones, to lead us in the Llysfasi yell!".

There was a gap before I could put my experience at Llysfasi to any kind of test. One thing it did for me was to respect the knowledge of those who produce food and raiment. Farmers are required to develop innumerable skills by employing their hands and their strength. Every day, some of the many aspects of farming must be attended to outdoors, and there are many jobs awaiting wet weather when equipment is repaired, sharpened or otherwise attended to.

The gap I mention was filled by a job my brother found when I became an office boy at a wholesale grocers in Liverpool. My future would be what I made of it. It paid £1 a week. Bills were sent out in handwriting - mine!

Soon I was asked to make a fire in the open grate, and boil a kettle. The head of the firm, Major William Williams, was the tea-taster for the firm. I would put 8 or 10 unblended piles of tea in front of empty cups. One teaspoon of tea was put in each cup. When I poured boiling water on each sample I would call the Major and he would raise a teaspoon of tea to his lips and pull it into his mouth with a drawn-in sucking sound. He would repeat this with a different sample. Inviting me to do the same, I would repeat what he had done.

"Now" he would say, "Number 1 is a cheap tea but when blended with 3 and perhaps a little of 5 we have a saleable tea and a reasonable profit." I knew from my first slurp that I wasn't going to be a tea-taster!

The next time I saw my brother Arthur I reminded him that he was going to speak to Uncle Jack. "Ah yes" he said. "He'd like you to call on him when you are free some weekend." This I did and I left William Williams and Co. three months from writing the first bill and boiling water for the first cup of tea.

3
COEDIOG

At last I found fulfillment. Uncle Jack and Aunty Mary gave me a warm welcome to their home, a farm of dingle and dell in the village of *Llandyrnog* in the Vale of *Clwyd*, North Wales.

Gone was the hurry and bustle of city life. I had commuted by ferry across the Mersey River to Liverpool each day, being bothered by a culture that puts up with a high density population. The change from my birthplace was enough to seek relief after three months, and the change proved to be among the happiest years of my life. I soon found myself sleeping well, working hard and eating heartily. This was a period when I was in prime physical condition.

Uncle Jack was a diabetic and for this reason his days of converting farm meals into high energy had left him. But he enjoyed life. Around 7 a.m. he would give me a wake-up call, then from his bedroom window gave William, the teamster, his orders for the day. It was time then for his early morning cup of tea. By 8.30 he was ready for breakfast, followed by a period of enjoying the prose of Charles Dickens. He had adjusted to his medical problem reasonably well. I often thought of Uncle Jack as enjoying favourite places. One was to take Toby with him to check the sheep at pasture. By noon, he had sent Toby home and he would proceed to another favourite place, the Red Lion pub in the village.

One of these favourite places was the least in favour with William and me, when we were ordered to the *Twll Tyfod* - this was an area of good quality sharp sand, in demand for building construction. It was our job to pile the sand suitably for the hauliers to load their lorries. But the sand pit played its part. For my uncle and aunt, the income from it meant vacations in exotic places like the Canary Islands and Minorca. Farmers in the Vale of *Clwyd* had no favourite places like these.

The little welsh ewe is the basis for farming in North Wales; she often produces twins but rarely triplets. Uncle would plan for a few January lambs. Lambs born in January and February would get enough milk to be weaned in time for about a month on lowland clover and ready for the Easter trade for welsh lamb in Manchester. If we could raise 60 pound lambs by April we would be satisfied.

Cosy in bed on many a cold winter's night, I'd be disturbed by Uncle Jack calling my name. Mechanically, I would light a hurricane lamp and head for the Dutch barn to check on lambing ewes. If they were having trouble I would help by pulling the lambs out of their cosy womb into a new, post-umbilical cord existence.

How did we identify the ewes that were due to lamb, to give them and their offspring the advantage of not having to put up with the rigours of a cold pasture? The plan for this started before conception. Before the ram is put with his harem, he is raddled. Raddle is a red dye made from ocherous iron ore and it is rubbed into the wool of the ram's chest. The dye leaves a red mark on the rump of the ewe when the ram mounts her. The first group of ewes to be identified we would mark with raddle on the wool between the ears, the second on the shoulder, the third in the middle of the back, and so on. In the fulness of time we would prepare the birthing place in the Dutch barn with protective straw and hay bales and the ewes that had it between the ears were the first in.

After a little experience as a shepherd, Uncle suggested that I should buy a flock of my own. He knew of a pasture to rent and I bought twenty-five couples. A couple in this context means a ewe and her lamb. My chest expanded in telling myself, "I'm a farmer now!" But my flock required little supervision. It was on good pasture and the lambs had grown beyond the precarious stage. Looking back I think the pride of having assets of my very own did not weigh more than the prospect that I was likely to lose money. Uncle's comment was: "You have to pay for experience." I can't remember details of the economic outcome but I think it was close to a draw.

At the livestock sales in Denbigh, Uncle Jack knew the farmers who kept cattle on hill grazing. The compulsion to sell on their part was because the mortgage was due or debt of some kind had to be met. They were selling less than half-grown cattle — or they ran out of grazing through lack of rain. The cattle were thin from inadequate nutrition but showed signs of good health and Uncle knew they would prosper at *Coediog*. But Aunty Mary was ashamed to have them where they would be seen from the road! "Mary bach, I'll move them to the bottom field after it recovers from taking the first haycrop then when I'm ready I'll ask you to pick them out among the other fattening bullocks and I guarantee you won't be able to tell them apart" - this in Welsh, of course.

At home at night I would be pleasantly tired but enjoyed reading, mostly history or historical novels while Aunty would read the British Weekly and Home Chat. "It says here" she'd say, "that the proper way to cut your toe nails is straight across and not on the curvature of the nail." I got to love Aunty Mary for her several good qualities. We enjoyed each other's company. After meeting my sweetheart she said she understood why I would be attracted to such a beautiful girl. She followed this with: "But you know, Trevor, she won't really make a good farmer's wife."

The only free time I had was on Sunday afternoons. I would jump on my motorcycle and head for the mountain above the Edward VII Sanitorium in *Llangwyfan*. Here, in the warmth of the summer sun I would read poetry and books to my fancy. Here it was that I discovered the magic and joy of reading. In particular, I liked "The Joy of Life" by E.V. Lucas, an anthology of lyrics drawn chiefly from the work of poets of that day. I also became interested in the Victorian author Wilkie Collins (1824-1889) and have become a collector of his works.

In Greek mythology, Mount Parnassus was consecrated to the God Apollo and the muses and on Sundays I would remind myself that my Welsh Parnassus awaited my joyful presence. For over 70 years this pristine place in North Wales has been my Mount Parnassus. More precious than photograph or picture, my mind's eye can still see every copse, every hedge and field, every brook and dingle. Then, for added pleasure of things heard and seen, there is the familiar "baa" of hundreds of little welsh ewes and lambs, dotted all over the mountainside. On weekdays I was the shepherd of my own flock, my Sunday muses still with me! To get to my Parnassus I travelled on a Roman road and there is a Roman bridge nearby, and "Helicon's harmonious stream", the stream which flowed from Helicon to the fountain of the Muses. Roughly parallel to this, another road takes one to the highest peak of the *Clwydian* range - *Moel Fammau*. From here the panorama of the patchwork quilt of the vale is in full view in this far-smiling land.

I was prepared for confirmation at St. Asaph Cathedral by Pink Willie, the Rector of *Llandyrnog* Parish Church. Cutting thistles in the rain was ideal for savouring the beautiful language of the Anglican Book of Common Prayer.

There are lots of characters in these Welsh hills and Pink Willie was one of them. He got married when he was over 60, to the Matron of the nearby

Sanitorium. A parishioner called to wish him well and was told by the maid (an old retainer) the happy couple was not at home. On a lighter note the parishioner said, "Please tell the Rector I hope all his problems will be little ones", whereupon the maid ended the interview by saying, "Oh, but the Rector is not that kind of man!"

The grand pastoral life suited me well at *Coediog*. Only once can I remember Uncle Jack raising his voice to me. He was trimming the hoof of a ewe with footrot and he must have cut to the quick. The ewe made a lunge and I was forced to let go of my firm grip around its chest. His mouth was close to my ear when he bellowed,"Hold it like a lion."

He could be a rogue on occasion. This vignette is an example. Road maintenance was done by a peasant, a barrow and a shovel. The road man was preparing for a bowel movement the other side of the hedge as Uncle Jack was passing on the road. He grabbed the shovel and put it under the perching peasant, quickly removing it and its contents. After a few mild groans there was contentment over a satisfactory movement, followed by expletives that sounded much better in Welsh: "I thought sure …".

I became a close friend of William the farm labourer. His English was no better than my Welsh but we understood the unfamiliar language more than we could use in conversation, and we got along well. He was usually jolly with humour evident in his facial expressions. Like most farm labourers, William suffered from rheumatism. It was an occupational disease through exposure to a cold and damp climate aggravated by inadequate rest. The body's defence mechanism in these circumstances had no chance against infectious agents that took advantage of a weakened constitution. Nowadays, we have antibiotics and anti-inflammatory drugs, without which pain killers of various kinds give only transitory relief. William rarely missed a day's work but he was constantly in pain.

Rainfall in Wales is sufficient to require farm labourers to work in it, otherwise the compelling jobs would not get done. The job I preferred in wet weather was cutting thistles with a scythe. I would use binder twine to tie empty sacks over my shoulders, over my head and around my middle. I would stay at it until the sacks became too heavy a burden to continue. I found the repetitive motions of this exercise freed my thoughts for silent philosophical discussion.

The symbols that meant so much in Liverpool meant very little in the ambience of *Coediog* or of my Parnassus. For me *Coediog* was a discovery. It was as though I had never known that the world had height or colour or sweet sounds, or that there was a special feeling in the hillside I frequented on Sunday afternoons.

My dominant feeling, if I can express it, was a strange new friendliness, as though this valley, these hills and sounds of birds and babbling brooks had spoken to me and caressed me. Working, eating, sleeping; in a sense I was a happy animal let out to run free. Not conscious of a quest for worth or worthiness, my uppermost feeling was happiness. From moments of high elation, however, I realized that my present contentment held little chance of survival. I had no capital to farm on my own and, in any case, the poor prospect of improvement in the economic depression that affected farming seemed unlikely to warrant a viable future.

I heard that Uncle Gilbert was planning to migrate to Southern Rhodesia (now Zimbabwe). The British government had started a program of imperial preference and this colony was found to have an excellent future for tobacco production.

It was agreed that I would accompany him. He had spent many years as a coffee planter in Kenya and he knew Africa well but he had brought his family back to Wales where he retired. The sedentary life of retirement did not suit Uncle Gilbert and, unfortunately as it turned out, he used his capital to start up farming in Wales. For various reasons, a slump in his assets made him consider a fresh start in Africa.

Uncle Jack thought I should have experience in ploughing before leaving for Africa. On a market day in Denbigh, over a couple of pints in the Bull Hotel, he was telling Uncle Will the plans for the migration to Africa and he asked if I could spend time on his farm, *Cae Drain*, learning how to plough. Uncle Will's reply sounds more in character in Welsh: "I'll see him in hell first!"

Anyway, nothing came of our plan. Uncle Gilbert decided rather hastily to accept a job as manager of a coffee plantation in Tanganyika (now Tanzania).

The unsettling effect of making plans and having to give them up was the first sign that my brief period at *Coediog* was coming to an end. It was too brief to call a saga but long enough to have an indelible influence on my future. My relatives were all farmers. Whether or not I had the instincts of being a good farmer would be for others to decide but I can say without hesitation that I felt at home quite quickly among the sheep, cows and horses at *Coediog*. It seemed to be in my genes and I was happy to have sampled the ambience that was the common experience of all my relatives.

With the present fashion for small families I wonder if youngsters today have a real understanding of relations. As a little boy I had dozens of them - aunties of all shapes and sizes and with fascinating illnesses. Like me my uncles all had plenty of hair, inherited from my maternal grandfather.

4
CANADA

In some ways, by 1929 the economic depression proved to be an epiphany for me. Government subsidies and lower prices in the market place gave some hope for the future. My father had left me a modest legacy at the right time for me to make decisions that I could afford.

My friend Ben Walker was planning to go to Canada and I decided to go with him. Accordingly, I consulted an advisor at the Canadian Pacific Railway Company in Liverpool. He had just come back from the Columbia Valley in British Columbia and he gave me an encouraging account of the prospects for fruit growing there. How could I effect a move that would let me test these prospects? He gave me the address of the Agent General for B.C. in London and soon I concluded arrangements to work at U.5 Ranch, Edgewater, and Ben Walker had a similar arrangement 15 miles north, at Brisco.

U.5 Ranch, Edgewater, B.C.

We sailed in April 1929 on the maiden voyage of a C.P. Dutchess, on the Saturday of the "Grand National" horse race and the OxCam boat race. Here's the first subsidy, the passage cost £10.

The flat-bottomed Dutchesses were built to sail on the St. Lawrence River up to Montreal but this made them vulnerable in rough seas. After leaving the coast of Ireland, Ben and I spent the first three days in our bunk. By the time we felt better we were hungry. Our luggage included a parcel which Ben's mother said was reading material but proved to be goodies to eat. Life began to be tolerable by the time we were halfway to the winter port of St. John, New Brunswick. I suggested to Ben that we should buy our rail tickets from the Purser on board to be ready for our land journey. Ben's reply: "Yes, you should. I know I've made a mistake and I'm going back on this ship!" Well, that was a blow, but I talked him into seeing the country from the train at least, before talking about mistakes.

I was impressed with the white tile of Child's restaurant in Montreal, but more so I enjoyed my first encounter with raisin pie. This was my order when we stopped at stations long enough to run to the food counter.

We travelled in a colonist car with slatted seats. We had no bunks or beds. The atmosphere became laden with smoke and the daytime picture was a constant wilderness until the early morning arrival in Winnipeg. After that the skies were blue and never ending. I remember remarking on the trees planted as windbreaks, making the farmsteads on the prairies attractive oases. At long last we came to Calgary with the promise of going through the Rockies - designed by the Great Landscape Architect of the Universe for the perpetual pleasure and refreshment of man.

We left the transcontinental train at Golden to change for the 60 miles trip south to Brisco for Ben and Edgewater for me. The Columbia Valley is formed from the Rockies to the east and the Selkirks to the west. Upwards of 50 feet of snow is recorded in a single season in the Selkirks and little of it melts above the tree line so that a thick cap remains on all its peaks. Precipitation is lighter in the Rockies, leaving the eastern slopes gaunt and bare above the tree line. Chinook winds remove the snow, leaving less water for spring run off than is needed for irrigating crops. Rainfall in the Columbia Valley is insufficient for crop and pasture agriculture, without irrigation. So farms appear here and there along the Valley only where the lie of the land is suitable and where enough lake water is available above it. Oh yes, the C.P. agent in Liverpool didn't tell me that soft fruits are not grown in this valley because of summer frosts.

The splendour of this place was to be my home for the next eighteen months. I left the train and met the rancher, Eric Smith, accompanied by a cowboy in a ten gallon hat named Bill Harrison. Bill was helping with the spring work and we shared the bunk house in the ranch yard.

The next morning I was ploughing new breaking with a wooden plough and an indifferent team of horses. I had never ploughed before. When the plough got caught on a root it tipped forward and lazy Benny, having been in the barn all winter, would stop in his tracks. Old Bill had been running with the cayuses in the foothills and was eager to go. I was pleased to have this frustration assuaged by the scenery around me. Just looking up gave me the heart to continue.

Let me just add a word in praise of the cayuse. This is the mountain pony, born and bred in high places with a wayward disposition and no more altruism than a cussin' cowboy. He compels respect over his confidence in travelling perilous ledges and he mimics the goat in going up and down the mountainside. It is beyond myth that a farting cayuse never tires!

Happy days at U.5 Ranch.

A few days after I had settled in I telephoned Ben in Brisco to find out how he was getting along. He seemed quite depressed and said he was planning to join the Web Bellis family in New Brunswick. Mrs. Bellis was a sister of Ben's mother and the family had left their farm in Mold just two weeks after our departure, to start a new venture, leaving the depressed economy behind them. Ben's father had a thriving business as a ships chandler in Liverpool. Ben had been to South Africa twice but I found no sign that he was ready to settle down in Brisco. After a short stay in New Brunswick he satisfied his desire to see Hollywood then went to Vancouver for a short while before returning home. Eventually he got married and settled down as the proprietor of a garage and petrol station in Anglesey.

Eric Smith took many a greenhorn under his wing at U.5, which was hardly big enough to call a ranch apart from the bush grazing. The acreage under cultivation was small giving rise to intensive production of vegetables for the hotel and C.P. Rest Camp trade at Radium Hot Springs, six miles south. All these vegetable crops were annuals and required irrigation. Occasionally, we would supply Radium with meat.

I remember a request from the C.P. Rest Camp for a suckling pig. We had a sow and her litter running in the ranch yard. Mr. Smith handed me the .22 rifle; "Shoot that son of a bitch". The young pig was processed, cooked and on the menu in the dining room that evening!

Apart from pigs, livestock production was extensive but minimal in numbers. We would use bells around the cows' necks to locate them and bring them home from the bush for milking.

Mr. & Mrs. Neville Hall had arrived shortly before me. They were an English couple who found their home country difficult after years in the tea plantations of Assam. They were trying out the customs and culture of B.C. and the likelihood of a stake in ranching. Mr. Hall and I were assigned the job of digging post holes and building fences around land that was being cleared. He was used to a feudal system where administrative skills and exercise of authority made no demand on one's energy. I dug the holes, he lined up the posts as I dropped them in.

It happened that my cousin had left Wales for the prairie the year before I came to Canada. He went to Edmonton when stacking sheives came to an end. He wrote to enquire if the rancher was willing to hire him. So Llewelyn and I lived in the bunkhouse and enjoyed each other's company. The going rate of pay was nothing for the first month, then ten dollars for the second, and so on, with thirty dollars of a maximum.

When it got to be 30° below zero, we would make a roaring fire in the bunkhouse stove before settling into bed, but by two a.m. water in a glass would freeze. Mrs. Smith took pity on us and took us into the ranch house. A stove in the living room had a stove pipe coming through grating in the ceiling for heating the upstairs and we could hear the Smith and Hall bridge game going on under the grating. Unbeknownst to me, the sewer system had frozen, putting the toilet out of order. Calamity struck when I flushed. Water ran over the rim of the toilet, over the floor and through the grating, to bring the bridge game to a halt.

The Thomson family lived across the Columbia River and their only access was through U.5 Ranch yard, then through the bush, and a row boat at the river bank. A day or two before Christmas, two of the Thomson boys were on their way home from Invermere where they had been celebrating. They stepped into the bunkhouse and left us a half empty gallon bottle of cheap wine. Llew and I were feeling homesick before they came so we soon started to celebrate, too.

By bedtime we were well on our way but managed to get to bed at the house, without incident. During the night I was awakened by Llew. He was having a vomiting spell. I was annoyed. We'd never had "words" before. I said, "You make sure you clean up your mess before you come down for breakfast." Shortly, he called me to the bedside and suggested I look on my side of the bed. Sure enough, without my knowing anything about it, last night's dinner was on my side, too.

After living at U.5 for a year I went to work for Eric Smith's brother who had an acreage across the field. I did chores of different kinds and I enjoyed the company of Archie Smith and his wife. He was constituency Returning Officer when the Federal Liberal Party called the 1930 election and in that respect he was at odds with Eric's wife who was a staunch supporter of H.H. Stephens who won that riding in the election and was in the Cabinet of R.B. Bennet. To my knowledge, Eric had no interest in politics.

The only other Liberal I knew in Edgewater was Leonard (Chap) Gaddes, whose father and uncle were absentee landlords and Chap as their agent was the most influential man in the community. He was responsible for ensuring the irrigation flumes were working and he ran a Christmas tree farm, exporting the trees to cities in the Northern States. The majority of villagers worked for him. By coincidence I renewed his acquaintance, 63 years after I left Edgewater. Shortly after I had begun working for Archie Smith I was involved in an accident which had a bearing on my decision about a vocation. It happened at a soccer match in Brisco. Llew and I were on the Edgewater team. I think I was playing inside right and I had the ball. Both Brisco players in the "back" position came towards me together and I thought this would be an easy touch. The plan was to kick the ball in the space between them, run around one of them, then I'd have only the goalkeeper to beat.

Woolfenden's big boot changed all that. He kicked me in the middle of my right shin. Diagnosis: compound fracture of the right tibia. I was taken to the Golden Hospital where the fracture was set and I remained in traction for six weeks, waiting for the healing process to be complete. An x-ray of my callus showed that the two ends were not completely articulated.

About 20 years after this event I went to an orthopedic surgeon, complaining of a chronic pain in my right knee. He said, "You have osteoarthritis and you must have broken your leg some time." Apparently,

A.B. Smith's Ranch buildings.

it had come about, as the x-ray showed, by the slight lack of true alignment in setting the broken bone. This affected the articulation of the knee joint, causing a chronic inflamation. On my daily walk these days, I use a custom-made brace on my right knee, which eases the discomfort of the resulting arthritis.

There was only one nurse on staff in the little Golden Hospital. When I was admitted she was on holiday so they had recruited the waitress from the Chinese restaurant as a replacement. I can recall with what amusement she assisted me with the bedpan! Lying in my hospital bed I had an opportunity for serious thought about my future. Ever since my days in *Coediog* I was tempted to consider life as a veterinarian so I enquired of a Vancouver newspaper if there was a veterinary college in that city. There was not, but I was put on to one affiliated with the University of Toronto and they were not sure about McGill in Montreal. My enquiry to Toronto put me in touch with the Principal of the Ontario Veterinary College, located in Guelph. He sent me a College Calendar and an application form. After reading through the Calendar twice I filled out the form and sent it on its way. The mail was slow but negotiations few and I was told to report for the first term of study on October 1, 1930.

As soon as I was able, I got used to a pair of crutches and was discharged, to be welcomed by the two Smith families and Mrs. Lee, sister of Mrs. Eric Smith. I shall always feel grateful for the affectionate care I received during my convalescence. The villagers in Edgewater held a charity dance in aid of my hospital expenses. I continued to improve and, though lame, I was ready to leave for Ontario in time for October 1st.

This ended a memorable period for Llew and me. It had been the first camera-click of our new home country but there were many snapshots to anticipate. We had worked hard and made good friends. The family and friends we had left in Wales tended to regard Canada as an opportunity to make money quickly, to return home for retirement and the good life. Here we were, on the first click already, happy with this as a home-country, yet eager to explore more film! We were on our way.

The Columbia Valley became indelible and beckoned me to return frequently. On the first of these with Llew, Mrs. Smith was living temporarily with Dorothy, her daughter, who was not home when we called. Unfortunately, Mrs. Smith had become older in mind than body. She didn't recognize us and told Dorothy, "I had a couple of old-timers for tea this afternoon."

The main links of friendship have been with Dorothy and her cousin Nancy Tegert, daughter of Mrs. Lee. Nancy lives in what she calls "The Old Corby Place". This is a small ranch in the foothills near Windermere.

The Old Corby Place.

36

She lives in solitary isolation in a log cabin, having moved from a large ranch on the west side of the river, where her husband was killed. His tractor caught fire as it fell on him. Nancy is an intrepid woman. We worked together at U.5. I am reminded of the time a team of horses panicked when she was bringing them for work after a lunch break. She was overwhelmed with their speed and, not letting go of the lines she was being dragged around the field. As this glimpse of rodeo was passing me, I jumped on Nancy and finally tired the team to a halt.

For 10 years, my wife Frances and I made an annual pilgrimage to visit Dorothy and Nancy. We would fly to Edmonton from Toronto, then in the company of my closest friend Edgar Graesser and his wife, Gwen, we began a refreshing holiday in Edgar's car. We zig-zagged south and west to Rocky Mountain House. Joining the Jasper-Banff highway we continued south, eventually leaving the Banff National Park to continue 90 miles on the Banff-Windermere highway to Radium Hot Springs.

The reunion at the roast beef dinners at Dorothy's each year were a time of happy reminiscences for all of us.

5

GUELPH

I bought a 1925 open Chevrolet for $175 from one of the Thomson boys. Llew and I packed what few belongings we had and started on our journey east, to Guelph, on September 12, 1930. If we had thought about the prospect for the old car taking us over 4000 km to Guelph we would never have started. But the exigencies of youth defy what is likely and we stay in ignorance until we meet our problems. Llew and I kicked the balding tires and jumped in to our new adventure. The road map said Calgary was 416 km to the east, a reasonable target for the first day.

Leaving Radium Hot Springs, on start of transcontinental trip in 1930, Chev 1925 with wooden wheels.

The Banff-Windermere Highway had a gravel surface at that time. We had become familiar with Radium Hot Springs - it was our opportunity to wash ourselves while we had only a bunk house basin in the 18 months we were at U.5. In winter we would wallow in the hot springs when the air temperature was well below zero, ice decorating the pool's edge with frozen water splashings. Radium was also the main source of economic support for the ranch.

The Gateway to Kootenay Park and to the Hot Springs is Sinclair Canyon, massive towers of red rock that leave just enough room to build a highway. Passing beautiful Olive Lake, the road winds through a changing panorama of mountain grandeur to Marble Canyon, so named for the white and grey marble of which its walls are made. The road continues to please the eye to the northern limit of the highway, in site of Castle Mountain with its impressions of manmade bastions and turrets. One and a half decades after I first saw it the name was changed to honour General Eisenhower but man's actions are less permanent than the mountain; now its name once again resembles its appearance.

Llew knew of a Welsh family in Midnapore near Calgary and we had joyous Welsh hospitality as a welcome. We soon got singing *Sawspon bach*, the nonsense song of Welsh football matches, then on to the serious stuff, *Cwm Rhondda* and "Land of my Fathers".

"So your fathers were brothers then?" inquired our hostess. "No, our mothers were sisters."

We explained, of the 4 sisters in the *Maesgarmon* family, 3 had unrelated husbands named Jones.

"Wait a minute, I've got an interesting explanation for the plethora of Joneses in Wales." Gareth our host looked up his reference which linked this to the Act of Union (1536) between England and Wales during the reign of Henry VIII. The Act required the Welsh to comply with the English custom of having surnames as well as Christian names. This became important in legal documents such as rights of tenure and titles to land.

To meet this requirement most Welsh people added S to their father's christian names. So William became Williams instead of 'ap' William meaning 'son of', which had been the custom.

Published at the time, by the Bishop of Lichfield, was this bit of doggerel:

> "Take ten," he said, "and call them RICE;
> Take another ten, and call them PRICE;
> A hundred more and dub them HUGHES;
> Take fifty others, call them PUGHES;
> Now ROBERTS name some hundred score;
> And WILLIAMS name a legion more;
> And call, "he moaned in languid tones,
> "Call all the other thousands - JONES."

The Trans-Canada Highway was not complete so we travelled through the United States, south of Lake Superior. Our first leg from Calgary took us through Swift Current where we had an unexpected claim on our thin purse. The car was left in a municipal parking lot while we had lunch. The windshield had been shattered with a rock, heaved over a wall. On to Weyburn, we found a park shed open in Estevan and spent the night there in company with mice running over us.

We entered the U.S. at Portal, North Dakota and spent the night at Minot, where I helped the ailing car by taking off the cylinder head to decarbonize the pistons and valves. The next day we headed southwest to the Minnesota boundary at Fargo. The long hill down to the Lake Superior shore in Duluth bothered the thin lining of my brakes and I noticed smoke from the left hind wheel. Not to worry, I stopped the car and put the fire out with a pail of water from the nearest house!

The trip through Wisconsin was a breeze and we went through Iron Mountain, Michigan then on to Escanaba for the night. A carnival was in full sway as we entered Escanaba, and we had our fortunes told by an aging gypsy. I remember her patting the area of her kidneys, telling me, "Sooner or later, you're going to have problems here." It is now 64 years later and I've been free from kidney problems. She would have been more credible if she had touched her right knee.

By this time we felt confident that the car would return us to the promised land. Patience was thrust upon us over a faulty oil pump which would overheat the engine at speeds beyond 25 m.p.h. but we had time to allow that to delay our progress. Michigan has always been characterized in my mind with the label, exuberance, even beyond what is generally found in this exciting country. This stems from its wealth derived from the auto industry, but there is also, in my experience, a lively enthusiasm for all that's going on there. I remember the State Governor at a Land Grant College Conference, telling us, "Why, we produce more maple syrup by accident than Vermont does on purpose!".

Now we were on our last day before entering Canada. We crossed the top of the State to St. Ignace, through the Straits of Mackinac, and south to the thumb, entering Ontario at Sarnia. We went to church that Sunday evening, as a fitting thanksgiving for a successful adventure. Llew and I were, finally, to go our separate ways. We had become very close friends. He joined the R.C.M.P. in 1931 and died in retirement in Victoria in 1983.

We reached Guelph in the early afternoon of the following day. The Scottish accent of the Registrar, Alex Shepherd, at the Ontario Veterinary College was as strong as any Doric in ancient Greece. He gave me a warm welcome and showed me around. "I'll be doing that soon" came to me on meeting the first professional, Anthony Augustus Kingscote. He let me see

Ontario Veterinary College

what he saw down the microscope and I had an urgent desire to understand my first glimpse.

Later that afternoon I was having difficulty entering the front door of the College with my cabin trunk, containing all my worldly goods. "You ca'na bring that in here lad". It happened the Principal, Dr. Charles Duncan McGilvray, having a strong Clydeside accent, was just leaving for home. "What's y'r name lad?" "It is Jones, Sir, I've come to start veterinary studies." We got talking and he finally helped me carry the trunk to a storage space in the college! Two Scots and an Englishman giving a welcome on the first afternoon overwhelmed this simple Welshman.

The capricious weather in Ontario can decide to let the Fall of the year be at its most attractive. So it was on October 1, 1930 that a frosty morning turned into a sunny day with long shadows. It was the kind of day that always puts me wanting to be ploughing easy turf with a well matched team of horses.

I was free that afternoon so I made myself acquainted with the buildings on campus. I've always admired symmetry in architecture, especially in small buildings. Imagine my delight in discovering the Old Grey Barn that matched what I was looking for. It was built in 1922 when the College was moved from Toronto to Guelph. It had a hipped roof and flat roof extensions, north and south. But good looks were not the building's only virtue. Over the years, what has lingered in my memory are the tones and

41

tints of smells that were airborne in and around the Barn. Children like most smells until they are taught differently, and some of us remain children.

In 1990 I heard that the Old Barn was to be demolished to make room for a new Lifetime Learning Centre. At this stage in my narrative I want to write a farewell to the Old Grey Barn, even if it puts things out of context.

On approaching the Barn the strange alchemy going on inside seemed to be producing a tertium quid, recognized by the coming together of aromas to form a distinctive new substance.

Each person has an odour as individual as a fingerprint - certainly, a dog knows its owner, even when he or she is an identical twin. So it is that a close link with animal species stores in one's mind the distinctiveness of odour, of horses, cattle, pigs, sheep, goats and rabbits. Each section of the Barn had odours representing all of these species. Then in the north wing, where Dr. R.A. McIntosh parked his Chevrolet, there was a pervasive, alien, synthetic vapour from the car. Clinical training was no more than 10 percent as brisk as it is today so the car was never in the way. As an aside, Principal McGilvray parked his car, night and day, on the clinic floor - where the stock room is now. He would remove it to accommodate clinic periods, three afternoons a week. In the classrom above the clinic, the last period on a Friday morning was pathology. Just before the noon bell rang we would hear the roar of the Principal's car backing out of the clinic and comment of Dr. Schofield: "The Principal is leaving for lunch with the Guelph elite, to discuss the better world of Rotary!"

But I digress. The most pleasant odouriferous delight in the Barn was on the second floor of the west wing where the new-cut hay with its heady succulence had been stored. It was here that my tour of the Barn had me musing over my recent past. I had left a ranch in the interior of British Columbia to enter OVC, and my olfactory sense aroused in me memories of the ranch and the sweet smelling earth, flowing from the cleaving share of the plough like some lazy wave on the seashore.

As I write this, my reverie is assaulted by reading about executives in New York who spend $50 an hour at the Hoffman Center for Holistic Medicine just for the joy of smelling scents of jasmine, sassafras and lemon! Unlike the vapours of the Old Grey Barn, these scents are not likely to cling to clothes.

The caretaker of the Barn, Joe Barnett, was a gentle soul. He lived in rooms on the second floor of the Barn. My classmates Swan and Hasson occupied the next room, and next to the rabbits. The pervading telltale with all of them was not the "odour of sanctity" but one well influenced by the proximity of the rabbits. I took Swan to my girlfriend's home, and she and her mother had to air the house well for a week to get rid of the smell of rabbits!

So I say farewell to the Old Grey Barn. In doing so I agree with Kipling: "Smells are surer than sights and sounds to make your heart-strings crack."

6

MY FIRST YEAR

The corpus of knowledge that characterizes professional people begins with the acquisition of the jargon that is absorbed readily by college freshmen. This elucidating glimpse came to me during my first year at the OVC in 1930. I found it a delightful surprise to make use of school-taught Latin in memorizing anatomical features of the horse during the daily dose of dissection. Jargon spilled over from anatomy into the judging course in animal husbandry.

"Doc" Staples was the king of the horse ring. My eager classmates would refer to the chest as the thorax, and I would swell with pride in discovering that the obscurities of science were largely a matter of language, and I was learning the language! This lofty position was in marked contrast with my experience in the previous spring, when I ploughed new breaking with an unmatched team. Agricultural students, whom we joined for judging should, I felt, gape with open mouths at such pedantry.

The College became the centre of my life's interests from the day I deposited my application in the little Edgewater, B.C. post office. Now, in retirement, the unhurried enjoyment of nostalgia seems to focus not on academic matters, but on the social mores of my classmates during our freshman year. The three years beyond the first were too bound up with serious studying to be part of a durable memory.

There were 35 students in the first year in 1930, and the seniors wondered how such numbers could be absorbed into the veterinary profession on graduation. The world was in a deep economic depression, but the richness and enjoyment of student life was unaffected by the dried-up hopes of most Canadians.

We indigents were given bedroom space in office rooms at the OVC at a rent of $1 per week, including the laundering of bed sheets. We ate and drank milk like calves at the campus dining hall, known as Creelman Hall, for $4.50 per week. The academic fee was $400 for the entire degree program.

My closest friends were a cross-section of the cosmopolitan make-up of the student body. Dave Hasson came from Kansas, Cliff Swan from Newcastle-on-Tyne, Ken Francis from Washington, D.C., Ian Macdonald Cruikshank from Edinburgh, and Willy Sutherland (known as the Duke) from Antigua.

Hasson misplaced my Welsh accent and labeled me "Scotty" Jones, the name that held for four years. Hasson it was who caused me embarrassment when, as president of the class, I was called into the principal's office. Again the Doric - "What are you going to do, Jones lad, about your classmate who refuses to acknowledge his part in giving a respectable girl morning sickness?"

The Duke, Hasson and I occupied an office, fixed up with beds, close to the principal's office. The Duke spent his weekends with old Dr. Cox, a veterinarian in Acton. He was never around on Saturday mornings when the bedsheets were replaced and his sheets became so dirty that Hasson sent them to the laundry. Returning late on Sunday evening, the Duke showed no indication that sleeping on the mattress bothered him.

Royal Agricultural Winter Fair time found us hitch-hiking to Toronto. Swan and I took the first vehicle to stop. It was a truck and we had a treatment of fresh November air. Shivering through Freelton, we saw a Cadillac approaching from the rear and, to our surprise, Francis was driving it and Hasson was enjoying the company of a blonde in the back seat!

It was arranged that we would meet in Francis' room at the Ford Hotel where he would repay a debt. Swan and

O.V.C. first year classmates, 1930.
From left – Francis, Cruickshank, Jones.
Rear – Swan, Hasson, Bodendistel

I were crestfallen when we went to the Ford to find no Francis on the register. We spent the night on a bench in Union Station. Francis had registered as George W. Styles, for whom he had worked as a technician in a Washington, D.C. laboratory. Giving his address a Canadian flavour, he stumbled over the spelling of Quebec Street, Gananoque, but he didn't stumble when it came time to walk out of the hotel without paying. "Scotty" Allen, a contemporary Aggie, quite innocently helped by carrying his suitcase.

Cruikshank and Francis rented a bedroom at Mrs. Lang's on College Avenue, next to the room occupied by Dr. F.W. Schofield, who taught bacteriology and pathology. One night, after imbibing a large cup of friendship between Scotland and the U.S., they got into bed. Cruikshank missed the picture of a dead fish which normally was the last feature he saw before sleep each night. They had stumbled into an identical house next door, rented by our English teacher, Professor E.C. McLean.

Dr. Schofield held bible class at 4.30 every Tuesday afternoon when he offered tidbits of religion in hunting for the souls among the arid student body. Cruiky attended regularly because he wished to be known as one who cared. He cared mostly about gaining a pass from Dr. Schofield during examinations. But Schof could not be put over!

One lab afternoon, I was surprised when Dr. Schofield told me that Smitty was at the door to see me. My contemporaries will remember that Smitty was the motorman on the street car that climbed the College Street hill. His quest - "Scotty, how about a party at the Royal Hotel tonight?" The party was easily organized, with the Duke and me co-registering at the hotel desk.

It must have been a successful party. I can recall Bud Fischer of the Royal throwing everyone out except the Duke and myself. Next morning when we were walking up the hill, Swan was approaching. Hasson told him we were in the cooler, and he was on his way to bail us out!

Swan was the closest of my friends. He was serious but with a sense of humor. He never touched alcohol and he worked harder than the rest, partly because, like me, he was ill prepared academically.

During one party splash, Cruikshank and Francis thought it prudent to stay in our room overnight - it was 25°F below outside! Cruikshank occupied the Duke's empty bed and Francis shared with Hasson. As soon as the lights were out Cruiky whispered - "Scotty, let's throw water on the Yanks." He had been heard of course, so the door was locked before he returned. In his underwear, Cruiky made a dash down College Avenue but, to his chagrin, he saw Dr. Schofield on the sidewalk. The chill was a match for Cruiky's antifreeze as he dodged from tree to tree, eventually to gain the next room to Schof!

In the early '30s, public interest focussed on the prevailing hard times. As an example of the deflation that occurred, my cash outlay for food for the entire summer of 1931 was $32! I should explain.

For the intersessional period, I volunteered my services, without wages, at the bacteriology lab and the poultry disease diagnostic lab at the OVC. Chickens, brought in alive, found their way into my cooking pot. I milked a cow for Joe Barnett in the barn, and he gave me eggs for collecting them. Milk, cottage cheese, rice pudding and custard got me through the summer very nicely, as I shared an apartment in the College basement with Mr. Twiss, the janitor. My diet was balanced with vegetables from gardens I looked after for the head janitor and for Dr. Schofield.

Twiss used to wash glassware in the sink while lab periods were in progress. He intervened once when Dr. Schofield was identifying a guinea pig with an ear clip. Twiss said, "Dr. Schofield, I think you are very cruel putting that thing in that little guinea pig's ear." Without hesitation Dr. Schofield replied, "Well, Mr. Twiss, I'm having a job dissuading the principal from putting a clip in your ear to differentiate you from members of the faculty!"

New college sessions used to begin in October, and among my most pleasant memories is the bright beauty of the maple trees flanking the highway in front of the OVC. In the middle of one afternoon lab session, I remember Dr. Schofield saying - and I hear it as clearly now as I did then - "Alright, forget what you're doing, it's time to marvel at the colour."

These are rich memories. All the classmates I've mentioned are gone. They are but a memory.

7
OTTAWA

To earn money for the next college session, Cliff Swan was lucky enough to have a job in the poultry department of the Experimental Farm in Ottawa. He asked me if the old Chev. would take us there, where he was sure there would be a job for me, too. There were no jobs.

I was given the telephone number of a blind Vet. in Westboro. He offered me room and board for keeping the kennels clean, doing the shopping, cooking the meals and doing general housework. I have always felt sympathy for blind people and thought of this as a satisfying prospect. The main source of income was a small army pension but he did reasonably well in supplementing this with fees from a few of his clients who had been satisfied with his veterinary services before he was blind. Unfortunately, his drinking pals knew the day his monthly pension cheque was due and a bacchanalia was always in prospect. The next morning he would look like death, lying on a couch. "Mr. Jones, if I die, phone the following people in this order." The sequence began with his doctor and ended with his wife.

Normally, the Vet. had the demeanour of an English gentleman. When he said two ladies were coming to tea, a picture came to me of hats and white gloves. He asked me to pick his ladies up at a downtown hotel and I detected they had already been in the sauce with little chance of balancing a cup of tea. "How much liquor is there?". I told them I had shopped for a bottle of gin that morning. "Only one bottle? You take us to Hull and buy us another bottle, nice boy!" Oh, my depleted treasury! First thing, when we arrived home, they undressed to their underwear and one of them was in bed with the Vet. The other was resting in mine.

It took me all that summer to read the Norwegian trilogy, Kristin Lavarinsdatter. That claimed my attention when I left the three upstairs. Eventually, there was a stirring and I went to see if help was needed. I could hear the Vet. snoring but the two ladies were in the kitchen area, which was on the second floor. In all, they had opened nine cans and made themselves a meal. I retreated to the trilogy. They both settled into my bed until I needed it. The Vet's mistress was awake when I entered my room and I told her to dress; I drove her into the city. When I returned, the Vet. was awakened with my sound on the stairs. "Who's there?" Me: "That's alright, I'm about to drive one of your friends into town." "Do you mean you have a woman in your bed at this time of night? You better get rid of her, and you can leave yourself in the morning. I can't put up with this behaviour".

I asked the lady to dress and I'd drive her to town. "I'll give you five minutes." Trilogy for five minutes then I went carefully upstairs, the only sound being the Vet's snoring. Instead of dressing, the lady was completely naked. I put her together as well as I could and gave her a fireman's lift downstairs and into the car. My host made no mention of these goings-on the next morning.

When he went on a fishing trip I was left as a quack to deal with the practise. A client showed me her Scottie dog with prominent lumps, which later in my college course I realised was very likely cancer involving the lymph nodes. The little dog looked distressed enough to desire euthanasia and this is what I advised. She started to cry and enquired about disposition. I said we used the municipal sanitary service for this. "You'll put little Mack in a box?" This wasn't usual but I remembered an empty butter box in the back yard, and with my best P.R. expression, I said, "Oh, yes."

"Then I'll sit with mother in the car and send my husband in to see you do the job properly." Sobbing, she left and her brusque husband seemed pleased to see the end of poor little Mack. In a similar case, the Vet. had injected liquor stric. so I did the same. The dose I gave was obviously insufficient. Mack jumped off the table and ran under the couch, with his master slapping his thigh and laughing merrily. The second dose did the trick and he left after I had nailed the top of Mack's coffin.

In the sequel, Mack's owner returned a week later to say, "I've been unhappy all week and I want Mack back to bury him in my garden." She was crying and seeking solace in her distress, when the Vet. returned from his fishing trip and with a voice reserved for his drunken moments, enquired, "Wash goin' on here?" When I explained, he contributed to the problem by saying, "Sush bloody nonshens". The lady appealed to me and gave me ten dollars to recover little Mack in his box. Fortunately, the sanitation man was happy with ten dollars and he recovered the box. Little Mack was given a respectable burial.

In most ways this intersessional period was wasted, excepting the extraordinary experiences when the vet's friends came socializing. At other times he rarely drank any alcohol.

He chatted with me about being a veterinary officer in the Boer War and life in South Africa as well as the many experiences when he was living in the southern United States. But mostly I was on edge having to be his eyes for people who expected a professional service.

Occasionally I would take an afternoon off. This usually found me in the visitors gallery at the House of Commons. I was still a naive immigrant trying to capture the cultural nuances of my new country.

8
INTERSESSION

John Storan was a broker on the Montreal docks. He was paid to recruit a crew for cattle boats. He was also paid by the crew - at least that part of it to which I belonged.

We sailed from Montreal, across the Atlantic, up the Manchester Ship Canal, for the people of the rainy city to enjoy Canadian beef. It was 1932 and students from McGill, Queens and Guelph got to Britain for $30. The foreman, Paddy Blake, was quick to find that I was the only student familiar with cattle. He and I tied up the whole ship load.

I can hear now the surging throb of the ship's engine; I can taste the dreadful coffee and the three-times-a-day mutton! It does not injure the truth to call the sanitary arrangements a monument of frigid vulgarity. We sat on a rail with the angry sea beckoning below!

But I must be careful. What after all can be more trying than other people's memories, unless it be other people's dreams? Too busy to be seasick, at night I slept on a sack of straw and dreamed of being home for the summer. I experienced a Welshman's *hiraeth*. *Hiraeth* cannot be translated from the Welsh satisfactorily - the closest would be nostalgia or longing.

I took the train from Manchester and went back home, having completed two years at Guelph since last I saw it. The summer of '32 is crowded with memories of cattle boat life and the Welsh countryside. I thoroughly enjoyed this intersessional period between my second and third year at O.V.C.

Cirrus clouds which looked like mackerel scales filled the sky in the late afternoon and there was a large ring around the moon that evening. A storm broke during the night. By morning clouds still covered *Cader Idris* but it had cleared nicely at the grey little town of Dolgelley — that is the way of the weather in North Wales. Indeed, haze and cloud are characteristic of the weather and more than this they permeate Welsh national life.

In spite of the prospect of rain, the day held great promise for me as I started off from the meadowy flats surrounding the town, on a hike to the top of *Cader*, which is second only to Snowdon in altitude. Arriving at *Gwernan* I made the acquaintance of Maurice Pugh-Jones who was enjoying a draft of ale. I joined him and we talked of many things. Revived by ale, bread and cheese, and conversation we started up the hawthorn-covered green slopes and headed for the easy climb to *Llyn Cader*. Here, slack with tiredness, a second revival was necessary before the ascent of the Foxes — the last thousand feet, which is a precipitous, loose gravel scree and a test to my lack of physical fitness.

The beauty of this place enthralled us. Mists were dropping down the hills into rain and later, a deluge. But soon, the grey day was transformed by golden light, revealing the beginning of a spouting stream — the *Dysanni*, glittering down from the tarn in a white trail, through the green, green valley to lose itself in *Tal-y-llyn*.

At that moment I wondered how it was that my ancestors had endured so long the hard life of these cruel hills - unless it was that they were trapped by this beauty finding it essential to their existence. The lure is there!

Maurice and I were absorbed in talk of the kind of country between the cradle's ribs of North Wales. Approaching from Chester one traverses the wide, shallow valley of the *Alyn* where I was born and where history records some of the sternest battles between Celt and Saxon. To the west the landscape is dominated by *Moel Fammau*, the highest mountain in the Clwydian Range. From its peak it is apparent that the Vale of Clwyd which lies beyond, while still an open valley, is deeper and not as wide as that formed from the River Alyn. *Brith Dir Mawr* is a charming old house near *Moel Fammau*. The house itself, lying where the wind chases the shadows across the mountain slopes, cannot be seen from anywhere! If you are lucky enough to find the poorly defined lane which serves it, you will be delighted with the peaceful setting of one of the oldest houses in the district. Nearby there is slight evidence of a road which is thought to be connected with the ancient Pilgrims Way. A coat of arms over the fireplace bears three human heads, said to represent three men who were beheaded many centuries ago. Yes, the pacific atmosphere in Wales is always turning up evidence of its turbulent past.

Let's continue westward into the Vale of *Clwyd*. Here's where I spent my youth, tending a flock of sheep and enjoying the grand pastoral life. Few places offer such an opportunity for bucolic blessings and peace of mind. "And over there," pointing to *Llangwyfan*, "is my Welsh Parnassus, of the happy days of my youth."

To travel west again from the Vale of Clwyd, into the highlands of Merioneth, where this account began, we find the valleys becoming narrower and deeper. Variety is the sire of pleasure here — lofty green hills, moorish pastures, gentle undulations as far as one can see. Change directions and all that is visible might be dim confused shapes, looming in slightly lighter mists. In these wild moors and mountains you can travel sometimes on good metallic roads, mere grassy wheel-ruts, loose shingle or slippery boggy mud. The calendar can insist it is summer but the elements belie the season. Heaven and earth can be so grim and splendid in their utter desolation so that you return to civilization, preferably characterized by an open, active hearth and feel that you've had a thoroughly enjoyable day.

The ancient Iberians were succeeded by the Celts as the early settlers of Wales. When Julius Caesar arrived in Britain in 55 B.C. the people were speaking the language that is native to Wales today. But these tribes of Iberians and Celts were never Romanized, as later they were never Anglicized. They peered perhaps with envy at the newfangled, modern equipment that the Romans introduced in the houses they built - such as the luxury of central heating and a hot bath - but as Rhys Davies has said, "No Welshman sold his soul for a hot bath!"

When a visitor crosses the border into Wales he soon recognizes a land sparkling with native activities. This little country has retained its ancient traditions, its culture and its independence because it has lost its political independence. It may well be that the energy that would have been used in dealing with the day to day affairs of state in a politically autonomous country, is used in my homeland, for national and cultural pursuits. Wales has produced more than its share of preachers, teachers, singers and poets. The Welsh language has been the medium for much of that which has been produced by them but it has become more and more apparent that there is a broadening stream coming from the Welsh hills and valleys that is enriching the vast river of English literature.

Dylan Thomas has gained tremendous popularity, especially since his death in November 1953 at the age of 39. He made a significant contribution to English literature. It is important to realize, however, that he represented and interpreted a manner of life which is essentially Welsh. Many writers of Welsh origin use the English language exclusively but they have been conditioned by a way of life created for them by long generations of ancestors who, from time immemorial, spoke a separate language and lived a particular and distinctive life within the protective aura of that language. One of these Anglo-Welsh poets, A.G. Prys-Jones, describes the characteristics of this group to include fluency, elaborate decoration, vivid imaginative power, quickness of wit, a verbal dexterity which produces a maximum emotional effect. These are the distinctive national qualities that the Anglo-Welsh writers are carrying across to the mainstream of English literature.

This little country of Wales is brimming over with natural talent in music and the drama. Every branch of music is represented in its repertoire. But it is in choralism that the Welsh excel. It is true that their native ability in singing harmony leads to a tendency for improvisation which may annoy the purist. Purism however doesn't bother the Welshman who joins his countryman for a thrill at Hyde Park in London, or when a group of colliers are returning home from the pit singing well-known hymns to chapel-taught Welsh words.

I am critical of my own kind, however, when I think of the incongruity that comes from being gifted in music. Not enough of my fellow countrymen reach the top flight of artistry because they will not devote themselves to the hard training and discipline that is necessary if a gifted singer or actor is to achieve the top rung. There are not enough good teachers and directors to bring about a high standard of professionalism. Meanwhile, the people of Wales are enjoying themselves with music and drama.

Country characters in Wales are a rich ingredient of the local scenery. John Hughes, William's father of my *Coediog* days, and a prominent friend in my *Clwydian* memories, was one of them. Chapel bred, philosopher, hedge-layer, expert sheaf maker, lay preacher and the rest, John Hughes convinced me that the supporting matrix of the Celt's fabric is non-conformity. Ideas were the real realm of John Hughes. I discovered from him that having ideas and not conforming went together. He was the living proof that formal education is not essential. I've mentioned earlier that many a Welshman can colour the truth in a public house on week nights as readily as he "speaks it plain" in chapel on Sunday, but John was not this type. He contributed to succeeding generations, the legacy that, in my young days, made the chapel the prime protector of the integrity of Wales.

Changes in the last half-century have put Wales on the map to an extent that was never the case before. Big business and all the political parties are conscious of this little country now. It remains to be seen whether the current wave of Welsh nationalism will impose a greater preoccupation with politics. In any case, these changes have been the cause of a mixture of fear and of confidence - a fear of being swallowed up and of being absorbed into the larger political pattern; a confidence that Wales is somehow different and can remain so.

Wales of course _is_ different. The world is conscious of the truth that this little country is compact of something much more tangible than the map maker's suggestion of a few regions tacked to the edge of England.

9
STUDY TIME

Returning to Guelph for my third year I was determined to become more serious in my study habits. My future depended on it.

I took a room and my meals at the Edgehill Tearooms, within walking distance from the college. Obeying a strict discipline, I allocated time for study and brief periods for play. Conditions conducive to studying required the window open, the blind pulled down and my sleeves rolled up. These lasted until winter intervened.

Following supper I was psyched up for action until 9 o'clock when I had two options: see my lady friend or invite my friend, a classmate, to listen to my review of the different subjects being discussed in class. The method I used in studying was to review and condense notes and reference material. Further review of the same material would reduce my notes by leaving out what I assumed I had understood and was now a part of acquired knowledge, unless reference was required to clarify the still misty aspects.

My classmate usually found poker more engaging than studying and he was pleased I did it for him. I profited as much as he did by using him to evaluate my hours of study. Another in my class, Ian Cruikshank, and I would attend the hops occasionally. They were held at the girls residence, Mac. Hall. Cruiky had become friendly with a faculty member at Mac. Once, after a hop, she asked us to visit the house of her friend, Gertrude Sorby. We had a welcome which encouraged me to ask Gertrude to be my partner at the next Saturday night dance. The date was fixed but not kept - by me. Saturday morning of the dance, I accompanied the football team to Western University. On that campus they have castor bean plants, growing as ornamental shrubs. Inadvertently, I nibbled at a castor bean without knowing that ricin, in the bean, is a very potent poison. It causes vomitting and diarrhea and may go on to symptoms of coma and death. The trip home was eventful, as I suffered the early symptoms! I managed to get home and to bed where I stayed for 3 days.

With much embarrassment I asked my landlady to phone Miss Sorby to tell her I was unable to take her to the dance that night. Naturally, she thought she had been "stood up"! I think it was on the second day I was well enough to phone her to apologize. The sick room had been well aired by then and I asked her to visit me. We enjoyed each other's company, the beginning of a friendship which got out of control; she became my wife. Gertrude and I had a happy marriage of 43 years. She died in 1976.

Andrew Smith was the Founder of the Ontario Veterinary College. He came to Canada in 1862, the year he qualified as a veterinary surgeon from the Royal (Dick) Veterinary College, Edinburgh, Scotland. The O.V.C is the oldest continuously operated veterinary college in the Americas.

Smith was given a private charter by the Ontario government and the first class of 3 men began in 1864. The lectures were given in the Agricultural Hall where, later, Woolworths nestled in the site of Eatons department store on the northwest corner of Yonge and Queen Streets in Toronto.

Smith's charter was surrendered to the Ontario government in 1908. By that time, 3365 students had completed requirements for the veterinary diploma.

The college came under the direction of the Minister of Agriculture and was maintained by annual appropriations from the legislature. Succeeding Andrew Smith, E.A.A. Grange became the second principal. At the outbreak of World War I the government was constructing a new veterinary college building on the southwest corner of Dundas and University Avenue, which was occupied in 1915.

Through affiliation with the University of Toronto, academic standards of entrance and qualifications for the degree was subject to approval by the University Senate, of which the principal became a member, *ex officio*. A significant reduction in students applying resulted from the effects of World War I and higher entrance requirements. In addition, a diminishing number of horses for city transport caused a declining interest in veterinary medicine as a career.

Principal Grange was replaced by C.D. McGilvray in 1918. Undeterred by the replacement of oats with gasoline, causing a decline in the use of horses, McGilvray's vision was focused on the future burgeoning increase in Canada's human population and the effect this would have on an increasing demand on livestock production. He was convinced that a large city was no longer an appropriate site for a veterinary college. Accordingly, he planned the relocation of O.V.C. from Toronto to Guelph,

60 miles to the west. In his view, clinical training would require the college to be where the farm animals were. His foresight and his plans became a reality when a new building was occupied in Guelph in 1922. Years later I was involved in a discussion about naming this building and without hesitation C.D. McGilvray came to my mind. As I write, the building is still unnamed.

In 1934, when I graduated, our degree parchment was handed to us by the Chancellor of the University of Toronto. This ceremony followed an evening meeting of the senate. We were to be in the senate chamber by 9 p.m. Sir William Mullock, the Chancellor, had forgotten us and the ceremony was about an hour late in starting. When it was over Principal McGilvray walked with us to Hart House where I, as class president, had arranged for a reception. The Great Doors of Hart House were locked but I managed to find a janitor who went looking for the Warden.

When he appeared, Warden Burgon Bickersteth disarmed me with three words: "What is this?". I explained that I had arranged for a reception.

"There is no record of such an arrangement. Hart House is closed." He retreated and we heard the great door being locked on the inside. This was a cold atmosphere for the farewells, following four years of living together. Most of us never saw each other again, as the law of unintended consequences started us on our professional careers.

My commitment for the summer of 1934 took me just a few steps from Hart House to the Animal Disease section of the Ontario Research Foundation on Queens Park Crescent. I was to assist Dr. Ronald Gwatkin with his research on Brucellosis, a serious disease of cattle. I was paid $60 a month, but the enduring friendship I enjoyed with Dr. Gwatkin had no price.

That summer went quickly. Head of our section was Dr. Seymour Hadwen whose work on snowshoe hares took him to the arctic in the Nascope. I was befriended by Dr. Murray Fallis, a parasitologist with Dr. Hadwen. Murray and I lived in a boarding house on Spadina Crescent and I well remember the rattling of milk cans at Borden's Dairy as an early morning call up, and the late night practicing of new recruits in the territorial army band in Old Knox College. Murray and I walked four times a day across the front campus of U of T which remains architecturally inviolate and untouched by the required expansion of Canada's largest university.

I was learning methods and techniques in veterinary research. The main experimental animal for our purpose was the guinea pig. Time has obliterated the details of the research but I remember well the need to take the temperature on upwards of 50 guinea pigs, three times a day. I remember, too, learning madrigals with the Foundation's choir which we sang at Hart House on special occasions.

Gertrude and I would meet on weekends in Guelph or Muskoka. We planned our wedding day and a new phase in my life began on September 15, 1934, with my good friend Murray Fallis supporting me as best man.

When I graduated with the Doctor of Veterinary Medicine degree there were very few opportunities for veterinarians to continue with graduate studies, and fewer still was the prospect of scholarships or stipends of any kind. The cost of pursuing a graduate program in the U.S. was prohibitive.

As an undergraduate I had heard of the recent establishment of the Institute of Parasitology at Ste Anne de Bellevue, a part of McGill University, and that the Master of Science was offered there. My preference was to do advance study in pathology. This was not available in Canada so I applied to McGill and was accepted for parasitology.

We found St. Anne's to be a pleasant community but, as the leaves and the temperature both fell, so did the comfort of our rented house. We would go to the movies for warmth! Our friends had an assortment of wires from the kitchen stove to their living room and this was explained by the fact that energy for cooking was cheaper than energy for light but it was silly not to do both from the cheaper source! It is easier to sin when everyone is doing it.

The title of my thesis was "A Study of the Bionomics of *Ascaris suum*". This is a common worm of pigs. It has a complex life-cycle. In preparation for my thesis I studied the body fluid surrounding the viscera of this parasite and was concerned with the fractions of protein, carbohydrate and fat as components of the fluid.

Shortly after commencing these studies I became aware that I was sensitized to this worm. No ill effects occurred on my first exposure but after a month's interval I resumed my experiments and in 3 or 4 days after this second exposure, I showed symptoms simulating hay-fever, which disappeared after a few hours. However, after 2 weeks daily exposure, there developed marked nasal and bronchial secretion with fits of coughing and sneezing. The consequent difficult breathing led me to seek the outdoors for fresh air. Asthmatic attacks and painful headaches developed in subsequent reactions. Experiments were discontinued for 3 weeks and when resumed, a reduced sensitivity was apparent. I sought collaboration with Dr. A.A. Kingscote of O.V.C. and he skin-scratch tested veterinary students with a 5 percent saline extract of pig ascaris which I supplied. We tested 108 subjects, chosen at random, and 27 showed positive reactions.

From the history of reactors we concluded that a period of exposure to the worm, but not necessarily by infestation, was necessary before symptoms of sensitization would occur, and that at least partial desensitization occurred through continuous exposure. We reported these observations in the September 1935 issue of The American Journal of Hygiene.

The Federal Veterinary Services held an examination for civil service appointments, the same day as McGill put on a ceremony for graduate degrees. I chose to be at the examination but it turned out that no jobs were filled that spring.

During the summer I volunteered to stay at the Institute, with the hope that a stable job would be found somewhere, and soon. My time was spent identifying parasites in the viscera of rabbits, sent in by wildlife biologists. There was no great excitement that summer. The economic climate was still in depression. A museum oriented occupation, grovelling in the digestive tract of dead rabbits to identify worms, had not entered my list of fascinating prospects in veterinary research.

Later that summer, Gertrude was invited to be matron of honour at a friend's wedding in Guelph. While there I went to Principal McGilvray's office. "So, you've got McGill behind you lad, what are you going to do now then?". With melancholy numbing my limbs I searched his face to see if he knew of anything. He did! "Only for the college session, lad, at $100 a month to help Dr. Schofield prepare for his laboratory periods in bacteriology". There was a smile on my face and a mood of celebration when I returned to my mother-in-law's home.

Technicians were a luxury that wasn't permitted at O.V.C. in the mid-thirties. Graduates could be had for a technician's salary anyway. So, I relieved Dr. Schofield of repetitive work required in preparation for lab sessions, including poured petriplates, and poured test tubes of different media for the growth of disease-producing bacteria, and other needs in teaching veterinary microbiology.

But I was soon responsible for the autopsies of pigs received in the diagnostic service and I assisted in whatever else Dr. Schofield was doing, including his research projects.

His cyclical moods influenced his output and his personality changes. On the up curve, Dr. Schofield showed signs of brilliance and made demands beyond normal expectations from those around him. The down curve found him extremely depressed, unable to sleep and think rationally. Throughout these problems he showed charity towards the poor and the downtrodden but this attribute was balanced by what seemed a constant campaign of criticism against those who in his opinion were shallow of rectitude. He was an iconoclast and he flashed the lantern of satire into many a foul corner.

Dr. Schofield is best known for his discovery of a substance in mouldy sweet clover, later identified as dicoumarol, which prevented blood from clotting. It thus caused a disease in cattle characterized by hemorrhages. This discovery later formed the basis for modern anti-coagulant therapy, used by people who are heart and stroke patients. It is also the basis of wafarin, used to control the rodent population.

It was during a wet spring that Dr. Schofield's keen powers of observation made him suspect a connection between the condition of the hay on farms from which we were receiving evidence of cattle dying with massive hemorrhages. I was helping him at the time with his research into this problem. We fed two groups of cattle, one with mouldy sweet clover hay, and a control group with hay showing no sign of moulds. He had me do prothrombin tests on the blood of both groups and this helped confirm that the clotting mechanism had been interfered with in the group being fed the mouldy hay.

When he published his findings, other researchers followed this lead by showing that coumarol, a normal constituent of sweet clover (*Melitotus albus*) is converted to dicoumarol by moulds and that dicoumarol interferes with the blood clotting mechanism.

His constant problems with lack of funds for research prompted Dr. Schofield to seek support from the deputy minister of agriculture. This worthy official was sympathetic and agreed to have a line item in the next college budget for $2000 to be identified, "for purchase of research animals". Some time later Dr. Schofield had occasion to ask the principal's permission to buy calves for his research. "Schof, lad, we have no money for that."

Schofield: "I thought there was a line-item in the budget for that purpose."

"Well, now, how do you think I paid for repairing the toilets on the bottom floor?"

Frugality was the cornerstone of Principal McGilvray's administration. He was known to turn back unrequired funds at the end of a financial year.

61

It was also a fact that for one year in the depths of the economic depression he operated the O.V.C. on a budget of $50,000.

His frugality was beginning to be troublesome for me. As much as we enjoyed her mother's company and appreciated being able to live in her home, my wife was wanting us to have a home of our own. This was only natural. When I went to see the Principal about this problem he had this comment: "I thought you would be quite happy under Mrs. Sorby's roof". After mentioning that I could not wish for a better relationship than I had with my mother-in-law, I said it worried me that my earnings were insufficient to provide for a house of my own. I didn't actually voice the implication that he was taking advantage of the grace and favour being shown by my mother-in-law but he knew I did not like being exploited.

Compounding this worry was the fact that I could not meet Dr. Schofield's demands without working evenings and weekends. Others before me did what I found myself doing in trying to predict the boss's special interests so that we concentrated on diagnostic material he was likely to follow up on, compared with what seemed less urgent for possibly several reasons. This did not always work and we would have worked in the middle of the night to avoid all possible confrontations and accusations of not pulling our weight. Relief came through a division of labour with a newcomer, Alex Bain, who had been our closest friend at Ste. Anne de Bellevue. I moved to pathology and Alex took over in microbiology. Alex and I got along well and it helped both of us when we grumbled about Dr. Schofield's being unpredictable.

I shall always be grateful for the opportunity to work under Dr. Schofield. It was harrowing at times but there is value in being exposed to a superior intellect. It is helpful too to learn how to control frustration. He taught me a great deal.

10
EDMONTON

In the early years of World War II, Alberta farmers were given an important challenge to meet the demand for exporting bacon when enemy action cut off the supply of Danish bacon to Britain. The challenge was to convert the plentiful supply of Alberta's oats and barley into millions of 200 lb pigs in 200 days. The sow herd was increased to five million in record time but there was less labour available because of the war and management practices and physical requirements did not keep up with this extraordinary expansion.

Here we have the single important reason for the need to establish a veterinary diagnostic laboratory in Alberta. There was as well a significant increased demand for poultry and eggs and from the present perspective it seems odd that the war brought with it an improved economy which increased the demand for ranch-raised fur-bearing animals.

In the Fall of 1939, J.R. Sweeney, Alberta Deputy Minister of Agriculture, visited the Ontario Veterinary College, seeking to fill a new position - Provincial Animal Pathologist. I met him on this visit, and shortly afterwards I received his offer of the position to start January 1, 1940.

I travelled by train to Edmonton between Christmas and New Year in 1939. My thoughts on this trip dwelt on the declaration of war on September 2 that year. Britain was busy with air raid precautions, distributing gas masks, rationing food and other business of preparedness. But this was the period of the "phoney war" - the fighting was delayed. On May 8, 1940, 80 conservatives at Westminster rebelled against Chamberlain and Winston Churchill became Prime Minister.

In the semi-somnolent inactivity of the train ride my thoughts ranged freely over the prospects of the future. Canada had declared war on September 10. Here I was on my way to accept a challenge which seemed more relevant than teaching because of this fact.

On the campus before I left Guelph the Officers Training Corps became active every day in the late afternoon. I was in charge of a platoon and I am reminded of the time I took it on a route march down the Hamilton highway just as the 5 o'clock traffic was leaving the campus. I had intended a march around the sides of a short square block, wheeling left at each turn. Alas, the first left turn was the sign to the village of Arkel, a mile down the highway. When we got to the sign I bellowed, "Platoon, stop the chatter and pay attention, L-E-F-T wheel." But Arkel was a mile up the road without a left turn between. My problem was that I had no experience in giving signals so I shouted, "HALT - AT EASE." By this time, dusk was upon us and I regrouped, facing a return to the campus. The parade was waiting for the lost platoon and as soon as we filled our space, I heard Major E.W. Kendal's commanding voice - "BATTALION, DISMISS."

On my way to Edmonton I met Mr. Sweeney again in Winnipeg for the purpose of ordering equipment and supplies for the proposed new veterinary laboratory. He explained that a fund of $10,000 from the federal treasury had arisen from custom duty, paid back to Alberta in the purchase of vaccine for the control of equine encephalomyelitis, bought from the veterinary laboratory at the University of Saskatchewan. It surprises me now to realise that this amount bought so much on my Winnipeg shopping spree! The basic laboratory equipment such as a microscope, steam autoclave, incubator, microtome and miscellaneous supplies were all bought for less than $10,000.

The new Animal Pathology Branch was financed out of the Horned Cattle Trust Account. This was a fund which the government accumulated by docking one dollar from the sale of cattle with horns intact, when received at meat packing plants. The purpose of this program was to encourage the dehorning of calves, but the livestock owners appreciated the various services financed from this source and it had little effect on the original purpose.

An empty space had become available in the Terrace Building, just east of the Legislature Building in Edmonton, and my first job was to plan the reconstruction of this space as a veterinary diagnostic laboratory. The space was divided into a general laboratory area for techniques in bacteriology and pathology, a post mortem room, a dark room for photography, and three small offices. The provincial apiarist occupied one of the offices and, later, we accommodated the dairy branch laboratory.

Government veterinary services in Alberta up to this time were provided by Dr. P.R. Talbot, Provincial Veterinarian. He functioned without the support of a laboratory. His main concern was to carry out field work in assisting the fifty four practicing veterinarians listed in the 1939 Alberta register. One of his main concerns at this time was to assist in the control of equine encephalomyelitis, which had occurred in epidemic form in 1938 and 1939. A vaccine had been developed by Dr. J.S. Fulton at the University of Saskatchewan, and Dr. Talbot was responsible for the distribution of the vaccine to Alberta veterinarians. He was also engaged in evaluating stallions enrolled in a registration program and he responded to requests for his advice in the field.

Clearly, there was a need for the livestock industry to have available the services of a veterinary diagnostic laboratory. The war time needs in expanded production of meat, milk and eggs brought this about.

In the early stages of providing this diagnostic service it became apparent that many farmers were not well enough equipped in management practices to avoid losses from diseases of various kinds. Accordingly, an emphasis was put on an extension service whereby preventive measures for disease control could be learned by large numbers of producers through talks and projection slides at village schools and community halls in many districts of the province.

In the Spring of 1940, F.E. Graesser was hired because of his expertise in photography and the production of suitable projection material. He developed a library of this material, which formed the basis for a winter program of visiting the various regions in an effort to bridge the gap over what was known but not used by livestock producers.

I recall on one of these extension excursions, my team mate was the Western representative of the Meat Packers Council. He brought three sides of bacon in the trunk of his car. One was to show what the industry was after (200 lb pig in 200 days). The other two represented an overweight and an underweight carcass. These 2 were actually docked in price at slaughter. By the end of a week of talks, the bacon and the hot stoves in the little prairie school houses had an influence on the odour of his car!

It was necessary to have good slides, clearly showing the message being given and the patter had to be practical and precise. I'll give one example. In the prevention of goitre in pigs, the slide spelled it out - "Put <u>one</u> ounce of potassium iodide in <u>one</u> gallon of water and sprinkle <u>one</u> tablespoon of this solution on the sow's ration every day".

Putting emphasis on extension service was a response to "first things first" during war time. However, we did not neglect two other objectives: a laboratory diagnostic service and the investigation of animal disease problems arising in the field. Four months after the diagnostic service began my report for the fiscal year ending April 1, 1940, records the processing of 809 specimens, representing 16 different animal species. In the next year we dealt with 1,457 specimens.

By the end of 1942 the Animal Pathologist's report included a plea for increased support to meet the need for investigation and research. Dr. Ross Walton was added to the staff. We were holding our own reasonably well but with one exception. We lacked the resources for following through when we had investigated problems on request of veterinarians and livestock producers. Several problems of economic importance were presenting themselves as the laboratory became better known. We did what we could within the constraints of time and resources.

Swine

We estimated that losses from disease and nutritional problems to be in the order of 20%. The simultaneous explosive increase in production with a decreasing labour force had an influence on this, particularly because many farmers had not raised pigs previously.

Infectious Rhinitis had spread to all regions of the province and it was found in herds even where management could not be faulted. The most serious effect of the disease was that it retarded growth. Affected swine kept under observation for a five-month period had made no more than an average daily gain of 0.35 lbs. We found that pigs exposed experimentally at 10 weeks of age did not become infected. The whole litter of a sow placed in contact with the infection when the piglets were one week old all became infected.

It was at this stage that we felt frustrated at not having proper facilities for controlled experiments and it was imperative to gain further knowledge on the nature of Rhinitis to arrive at measures for dealing with this disease.

Bovine Brucellosis

This is an infectious disease caused by a specific organism, *Brucella abortus*, which in pregnant cows results in severing the attachment of the foetus and thus causing abortion.

I had worked on this disease with Dr. Ronald Gwatkin at the Ontario Research Foundation during the summer of 1934. It was clear that the high incidence of the disease throughout Canada made a test and slaughter policy beyond a feasible means of bringing the disease under control. In several countries attempts were made to develop a vaccine and a killed culture vaccine (bacterin) stimulated antibodies but not protection. Thus, it interfered with blood testing as a means of retaining only non reactors in a herd. In 1940 the U.S. Bureau of Animal Industry reported the successful use of Strain 19 culture of *B.abortus* when injected in calves before sexual maturity. This was the breakthrough we were looking for. Accordingly, a certificate dated October 19, 1941 was issued by the federal Veterinary Director General to the Alberta Minister of Agriculture allowing the Animal Pathology Branch to supervise a program of vaccination. Within two months we had enrolled 10 herds in the provincial program.

A similar program was begun in all provinces and by 1954 the federal government acknowledged that the incidence of Brucellosis had been reduced to the stage that allowed for a test and slaughter policy, Canada-wide. Thirty-one years later Canada was declared Brucellosis-free.

Poultry

Avian tuberculosis was quite common throughout the province. Chicken offal was fed to pigs and to ranch-raised mink, and T.B. was thereby found in these animals. Free-ranging chickens were exposing cattle to the avian tubercle bacillus and this sensitized and interfered with tuberculin testing of cattle in the federal T.B. eradication program.

The wet spring of 1940 was responsible for a heavy incidence of Coccidiosis. Fowl cholera, fowl paralysis and laryngotracheitis were found to be present in Alberta flocks but these outbreaks did not reach epidemic proportions.

When commercial poultry flocks took the place of barnyard flocks, it was possible to avoid circumstances which allowed infectious agents to enter the premises. An exception to this was pullorum disease. The veterinary laboratory blood tested Record of Performance poultry flocks in a federal program. In the last three months of 1942 we tested 12,573 chicken samples and 636 turkey samples.

Fur-bearing animals

Our attention was drawn to the high mortality rate in ranch-raised mink in the Lesser Slave Lake region. A visit to the affected ranches showed clinical evidence of distemper which we confirmed by reproducing the disease in fitch, in the laboratory. We produced a formalinized autogenous tissue vaccine which controlled the disease in the following season.

Of interest was the development of tubercles in guinea pigs used for testing the vaccine for safety. The mink had been fed poultry offal and the tubercle bacillus had not been killed by formalin.

An outbreak of chastek paralysis in ranch-raised foxes was investigated and it was probably the first to be reported in Canada. This occurs when the ration is deficient in thiamin. In this case, the deficiency was induced by the feeding of Pacific coast herring (*Clupea pallasii*) which has the effect of reducing thiamin in horse meat. It was thought to have happened in this ranch during the period of pelting, when a day's ration can accumulate because of fewer animals to feed, thereby increasing the time for destruction of thiamin.

Another "first in Canada" was the treatment of impotence in a male fox with the synthetic hormone, Perandren. The rancher had an impotent male fox with exceptional fur quality. I was pleased to try Perandren on this fox and it worked well. The rancher understood my explanation, however, that selecting for quality of fur alone may submerge such factors as vigour, constitution and prolificacy and that I would advocate this hormone only in exceptional cases, such as the one on which he wished to use it.

On looking back at my experience as Provincial Animal Pathologist, it was a war time period of challenge and response. But by the end of the war and after a stint in the army, it proved for me to be the end of the beginning in establishing a new service. In 1947 I returned to the Ontario Veterinary College.

Postscript

In the Fall of 1947 I had a letter from Mr. O.S. Longman, Alberta Deputy Minister of Agriculture, to say that Dr. P.R. Talbot had been superannuated. He told me that a new position with the title Director of Veterinary Services would combine the duties of Provincial Veterinarian and Animal Pathologist. He offered me the new position of Director.

In the event that I did not accept, Mr. Longman asked me to advise him about suitable candidates for the position. Later, I was delighted to learn that he took my advice in seeking the services of Dr. E.E. Ballantyne, who was then Director of the veterinary laboratory in Truro, Nova Scotia. Events have proved me right about this recommendation.

11
RETURN TO O.V.C.

I cannot leave the West without commenting on synesthesia - that sensory blending, putting one into a delightful transport by bringing other senses into play.

When I see the word "Prairie", for instance, I think of long shadows of fall days, with never-ending sky, lit by bright sun. Usually the sweet smelling earth comes to mind as the plough share uncovers it, with the energy being supplied by the ploughman and his plodding team of horses. The single ploughline is lightly flicked across Madam's sturdy flanks while Boxer comes gently up beside her. The tractor breaks the silence of this typical October day, but the "wayawope" of the ploughman talking to the horses is easy for me to hear even now.

It is easy to bring back memories of rural Alberta, especially within the context of government services to agriculture. The contribution of the Ukrainian community dominates these thoughts.

I worked through the extension service of the department of agriculture and I acknowledge the help I had from Wm. Black and Peter Wylie who organized the farmers' meetings in schools and community halls where I met the District Agriculturists - with names such as Pidruchny and Chenasik.

We called Pidruchny "The Count" and his 6'4" commanding frame made his appearance appropriate to the title. A traditional story has it that he was approached by the 3 political parties during a federal election to stand as a certain winner in the constituency around Vegreville. He chose to continue serving his constituency from his office as District Agriculturist.

The "hiaminoosh" of the rail ties brings one back to reality. The train was returning me to Guelph, after eight years, during which time I had a stint on a secret project in the army. On leaving the army I had a letter from the Department of Defence which included "... that the secrecy ban on the entire organization and its work has to be maintained at all times and places …".

These memories turned my thoughts to O.V.C. and a watershed in the history of the Ontario Veterinary College began when Dr. A.L. MacNabb became Principal in 1945.

Principal McGilvray had managed to keep the College operating during his tenure of 27 years. However, the fortunes of O.V.C. were affected by two world wars, a serious economic depression and the need to adapt to changes resulting from Canada's post-war development.

The daunting task facing Dr. MacNabb was to expand physical and human resources for the influx of veterans who were taking advantage of war-earned credits. In total, 329 students qualified in the fourth and fifth years following the end of the war. In contrast, only 83 completed the course in the previous 2 years.

My return to the College occurred during this expansion process. I was assigned to teaching the laboratory course in histology and I was fortunate to have the assistance of Dr. J.D. Schroder. Our efficient technician was Ruth Saison. We occupied space in the dairy department building of the Agricultural College. From past experience under Dr. Schofield, I remembered how he could go from arrogance to panic, with nothing much in between, and I was relieved at the space separating me from him. Jim Schroder and I found ourselves just 2 or 3 textbook pages ahead of the students in our first attempt to teach histology. I had enjoyed this subject as a student and came to realise how important it was in the pre-clinical phase of veterinary education. Knowledge of the microscopic structure of body tissues leads to a clearer understanding of anatomy and physiology, as one expands into pathology, medicine and surgery.

We prepared class sets of slides of different tissues and found ourselves in a cooperative mood trying to avoid panic in keeping up with the daily influx of veterans, with a serious purpose, preparing to enter an honorable profession.

In addition to teaching histology, Dr. MacNabb gave us a field project to determine the value of different biological products in attempting to control infectious rhinitis in swine. This took us into Waterloo County to visit farms for this purpose, when we were not required to teach.

I was also involved with Dr. A.F. Bain, on assignment, to attend sales of army surplus with instructions to purchase whatever seemed useful in meeting a lack of space, furnishings and equipment at the College. We bought portable huts, tables, counters, and stools to be used in temporary teaching laboratories. Our list of needs were met from various sources and we were given our freedom to shop around.

A noticeable difference was taking place between the two colleges on campus. At the Agricultural College a new President, Dr. W.R. Reek, showed a friendly mood for cooperation with O.V.C. which had been lacking. Veterinary students now enjoyed full use of facilities for physical education, cultural and other extra-curricular programs. All campus personnel were given free veterinary services at the pet clinic at O.V.C. Events for social contact throughout the campus were being encouraged.

Previous to his appointment to Guelph, Dr. MacNabb had been Director of Laboratories at the Ontario Department of Health for 17 years. He had been equipped with administrative experience that served well during the virtual revolution, changing O.V.C. into a lively, dynamic institution during the five short years of his tenure.

In July 1950, Dr. MacNabb showed signs of ill health and soon afterwards he was hospitalized with a tumor of the brain.

I was called into the Ontario Minister of Agriculture's office. Col. T.L. Kennedy greeted me with a firm handshake.

"This is a great tragedy," was his first comment. "I have been very interested and pleased over the rapid expansion at the Veterinary College and my appointment of Dr. MacNabb as Principal, five years ago, has given me a lot of satisfaction." He used the collective "we" in voicing his support that the program at Guelph must not lose the momentum given to it during Dr. MacNabb's tenure.

He shifted direction: "I understand you are a Welshman."

"Yes sir, and proud of it." As soon as I had replied I thought I had said the wrong thing but no, Col. Kennedy said, "That's good, I like a man to be proud of his roots."

"I saw Dr. MacNabb in hospital yesterday, and he was surprisingly cheerful. He recommended that you act in his place during his illness, that's why I brought you here today."

Returning to Guelph, I went to see Dr. MacNabb. He gave me a welcome as though I were the patient and he said, "Do your best, I won't be looking over your shoulder."

The future of the College was uncertain but faculty and staff made it easier for me by seeming to understand my position.

During the two years I was acting principal I pondered over the directions that should be taken. My mandate was to mind the shop but I had no authority to implement any significant changes.

The period was 1950-1952 and post-war challenges were still being championed. So far as the flexibility of budgetted funds would allow, I tried some changes to the program.

From my student days, I realized that Principal MacGilvray had not understood the value of research to a teaching institution and he seemed to harbour a preference for incestuousness in the group of teachers he had under him. All but one when I was a student had qualified at O.V.C.

Dr. MacNabb arranged for part-time instructors from the School of Hygiene, University of Toronto, and he used radiologists and other medical specialists in private practice or in salaried positions to meet the need of teaching the large classes of veterans.

This was the beginning of a policy acknowledging that new ideas and new techniques result from assembling academics from a variety of institutions.

I got agreement from heads of departments that we should try to attract foreign veterinarians to spend time with us. We used the title Graduate Assistant and we were surprised at the response when we offered temporary appointments at a stipend of $3600 per annum. They came to us from the U.S., the U.K., Australia, New Zealand, Denmark and other countries. Our net had caught a group of venturesome young people to transform us into a mini U.N.!

Enquiring minds surfaced from this group and we were soon experiencing the embarrassment that a stipend is a fraction of the cost of worthwhile research.

Meanwhile, Dr. MacNabb's health deteriorated and he died on February 16, 1952.

12

THE DEAN

In March 1952 I became Principal of O.V.C., made vacant by the death of Dr. MacNabb.

Two years as Acting Principal had given me experience in dealing with administrative processes but the immediate challenge would be to continue Dr. MacNabb's policy of expansion, not only dealing with increasing numbers of students but also to identify some weaknesses, with the view to improving different aspects of the program.

This account is not to serve as a history of O.V.C. Indeed, I have no capacity to deal with the comprehensiveness and objectivity required of the historian. I intend to record selective events in which I have had a special interest, but it will be easy, after being retired for more than 25 years, for the frailties of prejudice and bias to surface. It is impossible to be scrupulously accurate about facts. However, I trust the narrative will be guileless.

What interesting statistics are there about the College in 1952? O.V.C. had been in continuous operation for 90 years and during that period, 5, 551 students had graduated by the spring convocation that year. In September, 272 students had registered. The professional staff numbered 59, the non-professional, 100.

Dr. J.A. Henderson had long wanted to see a farm service group attached to his Department of Clinical Studies. Accordingly, in 1953 we invited veterinarians within a practicing radius from the College to a meeting. We announced our plans to begin an ambulatory clinic, answering calls to farms in a regular veterinary service. It would be made clear to our clients that supervising clinicians would require students to carry out certain procedures on the farmer's animals. Our objective was to improve our clinical training program. We would charge the prevailing fees for our service.

In the outcome we retained good relations with neighboring veterinarians, and students benefitted from this program. Faculty members in other departments also became involved when ambulatory clinicians referred interesting cases of animal diseases to them, depending on their special field of research or investigation.

In 1949 Dr. MacNabb had purchased a 46 acre farm close to the College, to serve as an experimental research station. It had not come into use through pressure from other concerns. By 1953 we were ready to form a Committee On Research and this started demands for construction of prefab. buildings at this site. The Committee also encouraged faculty members to apply for financial assistance from the National Research Council and other granting agencies. Our research program was expanding.

Meanwhile, I was invited to join the Executive Board of the Chicago-based American Veterinary Medical Association (AVMA) as successor to Dr. MacNabb on that body. My main interest here was the Association's Council On Education, which operated a program on accreditation of veterinary colleges in the U.S. and Canada. Accrediting teams were selected to visit about 8 colleges a year. This was an excellent way to compare our program with others. In addition, I was chosen on two occasions by the umbrella organization to visit as a team member, in carrying out an assessment of the entire university program at Cornell University and at the University of Georgia. I believe accreditation has done a great deal to elevate the standards of post-secondary education in the U.S. It is a voluntary service and had not been used by Canadian universities to the same extent.

Our research program had expanded by this time, to the point that we needed a graduate studies program. The University of Toronto offered two post-graduate degrees in our area, neither of which attracted many candidates. The Master of Veterinary Science had been offered for many years but Tom Batt was the only candidate to apply. The Doctor of Veterinary Science could be obtained by submitting a thesis, without resident study, and this had appealed to a number of our graduates, but the M.V.Sc. required resident study on the home campus in Toronto, with no credit for study at Guelph. The trouble was that potential candidates other than Tom Batt could not find supervisors on the Toronto campus who were knowledgeable about veterinary science.

Toronto's Dean of the School of Graduate Studies was Andy Gordon. I met him at his office. He was head of chemistry - the deanship was a part-time job. I explained that we had several suitable supervisors for graduate students, doing first rate research in fields that would attract veterinary students wishing to pursue further study beyond the D.V.M. degree. The university should allow credit for resident study at Guelph.

"Shall I tell you the problem?" he said, and continued with another question. "Who appoints members to your faculty?" I replied that it was within my responsibility. Then he amazed me by asking, "But where does the money come from?" I said, "Like yours, the main source is the Ontario government." I could only assume he was insisting that the President through the Senate needed to appoint faculty members who supervised graduate students. The terms for affiliation with the University of Toronto did not include the hiring of O.V.C. members of faculty.

Later, in a brief discussion with President Sidney Smith, I explained that we wanted the university to allow credit for resident study at Guelph. He said, "I'll put Claude on to you."

Claude Bissell was vice-president, assisting the president in the resolution of problems. He was a facilitator. He understood our problem and offered to accept my suggestions. The university appointed a committee to visit O.V.C. to become acquainted with the research underway and to meet the scientists involved, who were the prospective supervisors of candidates applying to the School of Graduate Studies to meet requirements for the M.V.Sc. degree. The committee carried out its mandate and by 1956 the Master's program was available by resident study at Guelph.

More on Tom Batt. His father was the best teacher we had in my student days. Tom qualified in 1933, one year ahead of me.

I feel sure, living in the sixteenth century would have appealed to Tom. I can visualize him in silken breeches and a doublet, writing sonnets and helping vista-gardeners as a member of Good Queen Bess's Court. His hobby was creating vistas with columns and conifers in the most elaborate garden in Guelph.

Following graduation Tom acquired two degrees with resident study in Toronto, two degrees at Cornell, then one in Paris. He returned to Guelph to take over the teaching of physiology. I think he mimicked his mentor, Prof. Dukes of Cornell, author of the definitive book on veterinary physiology. The first lab. period in a new session, Tom would lay down the law. No student shall enter the laboratory without wearing a clean, white lab. coat. He warned that every student, on the second lab. period, shall have before him, Dr. Duke's text-book, with his name written therein. He would then clarify the student's responsibility - "You are responsible for every word on every line of every page of the text-book". His voice was articulate and it projected well. He had clarified in each student's mind the rules for success in his subject.

A major problem arose with Tom. While he had changed physiology from being the poorest taught subject to the best taught, and in spite of having completed, successfully, six university degrees, he closed the book on research; he would have none of it.

My involvement with the AVMA on accreditation had shown me the importance of research in physiology. Indeed, it was *sina qua non* for the enrichment of our research program. I was influenced here by the burgeoning subjects of cellular biology, genetics, blood-cell research and all those areas bridging the gap between structure and function. Tom could not be allowed to confine the Department of Physiology to an undergraduate teaching program.

After several changes aimed at a satisfactory accommodation to the administrative aspect of this problem, the final outcome, in 1957, was to create a new department, responsible for teaching and research in physiology, pharmacology, anatomy, histology and embryology, cellular biology, including cellular genetics. We called it the Department of Biomedical Sciences. Dr. H.G. Downie was appointed Professor and Head of the department.

By 1957 the total faculty numbered 66. Twenty-five of them had been given leave-of-absence without pay for educational purposes. Our policy to develop a teaching staff with diverse experience and training was successful, and by 1957 degrees from the following universities were represented among our members of faculty: Bristol, Edinburgh, Glasgow, Liverpool, Manitoba, McGill, McMaster, Pretoria, Queen's, Saskatchewan, Sydney, Toronto, Western Ontario, Alfort, Belgrade, Colorado, Cornell, Illinois, Iowa, Michigan, Minnesota and Wisconsin.

In 1959 a new Medical-Surgical Building to house the Department of Clinical Studies was opened in an Official Ceremony. This included a teaching hospital. It is not generally realized that veterinary education has a requirement for a capital fund to build its own hospital for use in clinical training. Dr. J.A. Henderson, head of the department, was the prime mover for this building. He and I joined the faculty in 1947. Jim was well known for having established the first clinic for bovine artificial insemination. This was in New Jersey. He is best known as the co-author of a text book with D.C. Blood titled "Veterinary Medicine," first published in 1960.

Celebrating O.V.C.'s Centenary in 1962.

13

INDIA

Browsing through passports releases the magic power of remembering journeys past. My job has not taken me to China or what was the U.S.S.R., but I've been to just about all the other regions of the world.

It all began in 1955. I was put on an expert panel on veterinary education, created by two U.N. Agencies, the Food and Agriculture Organization (FAO) and the World Health Organization (WHO).

My first trip in international development took me around the world. This began by attending a conference on animal diseases in the tropics, held in Brisbane, Australia.

Delegates from 15 countries attended this conference; I only knew one, Dr. J.G. Black, a 1942 graduate of O.V.C., who was stationed in Northern Rhodesia at that time.

Trevor as rappaaorteur, with Sir John Ritchie, Chairman, at meeting of Expert Panel, F.A.O., Rome

Where control programs are not well organized, Rinderpest, a disease of cattle, causes heavy losses. At that time it was reported to be widespread in Viet Nam, Cambodia, Laos, Burma, India and Pakistan. Outbreaks were rare in Afghanistan, while Malaya, Singapore, Sri Lanka and Iran were free. The Philippines had been free for some time but had controlled an outbreak just a month before the conference. Rinderpest was eradicated in Thailand in 1948 but the occasional outbreak occurs by extension from Cambodia and Laos. Many other diseases were of less importance in most tropical countries but Hemorrhagic Septicaemia was reported as the greatest economic loss from disease in cattle in the tropics, north of the equator. Interesting in this regard is that predisposing conditions such as cold rains in the monsoon season, especially when combined with a period of low nutrition, trigger an outbreak. Also, eating the first green shoots after the monsoon will cause scouring which will precipitate an outbreak. FAO has been successful in initiating campaigns for control of livestock diseases in several developing countries.

Seeing tropical Queensland and the Northern Territory from the air, in a flight from Brisbane to Darwin, revealed for a Canadian an unusual flora and topography. Fires in the unoccupied bushland south of Darwin created a fairyland appearance from the plane. It was a reminder of loss of a valuable resource, common to Australia and Canada.

From Darwin I flew to Djakarta on my way to Singapore where I spent an interesting week as the guest of the Chief Veterinary Officer. Here and in Malaya I was impressed with the way British veterinary officers in the Colonial Service were training indigenous veterinarians to take over, in preparation for self-government.

On arrival in Bangkok I met Sir Thomas Dalling, leader of a team on our way to India to advise on the training of personnel for the veterinary services of that country. Before leaving Thailand we visited the veterinary college at Bangkok, then travelled over 100 miles through the jungle to Packchong where, under the guidance of FAO, vaccines against animal diseases were prepared and used on livestock in several countries in the area.

Word had got out that strangers were visiting the laboratory at Packchong. Our hosts had arranged for dinner outside on a large patio and the villagers sat around the periphery watching these strange people eat. After the meal the villagers put on a dance. The orchestra was made up of 8 or 10 boys, each of them having a different size piece of metal threaded on a string. They allowed the metal to fall on another piece, thereby achieving a dance rhythm when they took turns to make a sound by metal falling on metal. The dancing couples did not face each other. Instead, boy followed girl while girl did things to her fingers, flexing them backward in motions both graceful and artistic. Boy did similarly but with less grace.

Sir Thomas beckoned me: "I want you to get in line with that pretty girl."

I would be the only European on the dance floor making a fool of myself so I said, "If you will take a partner too."

"No", said he, "I've found a young lady who does the waltz and we're going to give a demonstration when this is over."

I did what I was told but soon got fed up looking at the pretty girl's back. I took a step in front of her and tried the finger moves in front of her pretty face. That brought the dance to a halt! Sir Thomas delighted all present with the sensible steps of the waltz, even though the music came from a scratchy record played on an old wind-up gramaphone. What a refreshing entertainment in the midst of a tiger and snake jungle, where we were told we'd be wise not to take a jungle walk.

Now on to Delhi where the rest of the mission had arrived from the other way. There were three Scots and one from each of the following - Australia, England, Switzerland and Canada. Two officers of the British Colonial Service joined us, one from Sri Lanka, the other from Malaysia.

Before meeting senior officers of the Indian government we indulged a personal need. We all got fitted for a white tropical jacket and trousers. They were delivered to our hotel the following day!

At the request of the Indian government, FAO of the U.N. arranged for this team of experts to visit several veterinary colleges in India and to participate in a seminar with Indian veterinarians for the purpose of appraising veterinary education and making recommendations with respect to the need for training personnel for the veterinary services of that country.

Conferences with these National Government Officers were crucial to a helpful outcome from this exercise. In India, education is under the jurisdiction of each state but loans and grants from such agencies as the U.N., the several sources of loans under the World Bank, and grants from private foundations require the blessing of the Indian government.

Indian officials we met in Delhi were a foil for our individual opinions that had developed from completely different parameters. It was refreshing for me to find evidence of a high standard of statecraft in this newly independent country.

My team colleague from Australia and I seemed to understand the reason for caution expressed occasionally by the host country over the fact that governance, like Canada's, was less centralized than that in the British tradition. In these circumstances, a political element was essential for the team to consider. This perhaps became the least of the team of experts' expertise! It need not be emphasized that culture and tradition were constant reminders of the differences that prevailed.

More important for the team was the difference in the way veterinary services are delivered in tropical countries. In the temperate zones where, by and large, endemic diseases have been controlled, individual animals have an economic value that justifies veterinary intervention, whereas the prevalence of epizootics in tropical countries require control measures on a herd and flock basis. Because of these differences, the education and particularly the clinical training in these two zones require an important difference in emphasis. In temperate zones many infectious diseases of animals are of historical interest only, whereas they must be dealt with thoroughly in the education programs of veterinarians involved in controlling them in the tropics.

We visited veterinary colleges in Mathura, Patna, Calcutta, Madras, Hyderabad and Bombay.

I developed the usual bowel problem of the tropics before leaving Delhi for Mathura in Uttar Pradesh and was utterly miserable for the entire visit, mostly from dehydration. It was planned that we would see the Taj Mahal on our return to Delhi. This I was not going to miss. Close to Agra our wall-eyed Sikh driver made a lurch around a corner. Just in time, he had noticed a camel train occupying most of the narrow road.

Before we could catch our breath - there was the Taj Mahal, the most splendid specimen of mogul architecture to be found anywhere. It was built by Shah Jahan as a mausoleum for his wife. Exquisitely elaborate carving, pointed arches and minarets are all represented. This wonder of the world was just what I needed to remove my malaise. We left the Taj and eventually arrived at the train station in Delhi.

An overnight train journey got us to Patna in the poverty-stricken state of Bihar. An eager group of college teachers were doing their best, with very few resources. We encouraged them in seeking financial assistance to send bright young members of faculty to take graduate study appropriate to the discipline for which they were suited. I recall the last session with senior faculty when circumlocution made it difficult for us to express frank opinions about sending professor X to gain an expertise in virology and professor Y for exposure to the excellent program on epidemiology at Davis, California. Our promise was to help bring such assistance to pass. We also discussed the notion that in our opinion there were properly motivated and well-trained young veterinarians in different world regions who would consider it an opportunity to be useful to mankind in spending time at the Patna Veterinary College.

A national problem in India is the 'stay at home' mentality. There is little sense of adventure which would require a change of domicile even locally and less, from one state to another. This attitude is understandable among the poor who have a job and think about the risks attendant to any move that could go wrong. It might put them and their family into greater poverty by having expressed a foolish desire to improve their lot. 'What we have, we'd better hold' was the common attitude.

I remember well the personal discomfort at the hotel in Patna. There was an ancient air conditioner in the window of my bedroom. When it was on I could not sleep for the noise of the fan. When I turned it off I discovered it had served, whilst on, to keep mosquitoes out of the room. On or off, there was no possibility of sleep.

The mission left Patna by air, to Calcutta. Arriving in Dum Dum airport we travelled the Barrackpore Trunk Road into the city. On each side of the road, in the black of the night, there seemed endless movement of white-clad pedestrians. Where were they going? Behind these were the hovels of those well enough off to have a roof over their head. The movement from East Bengal during partition caused an insoluble problem with refugees and here they were. Most had no shelter, sleeping on rope cots. Cattle roamed freely through this multitude and heaps of refuse were scattered everywhere. Poverty is much more visible in an urban setting than it was in Bihar.

The Bengal Veterinary College in Calcutta had better equipment than Patna but the teachers needed to be trained to a higher standard for them to make use of more sophisticated equipment to improve the quality of education.

On to the state of Tamil Nadu and its capital of Madras where sunn, a tough hemp and some finer fibers were first developed. Here we found a relatively enlightened group of educators and a self-styled notion that this can be expected, as one travels south in the subcontinent. Here it was too that we heard of the female graduate student who had been at a conference in Delhi and had asked good questions of a male lecturer at the end of a somewhat esoteric presentation. The lecturer was impressed by the questions. A private conversation ensued and this led to a lively correspondence about the left-hand bottom corner of the symbol for a complex chemical compound! Then came the time she added a postscript in one of her letters: "I am not married", which amounted to a proposal. They have lived happily - he's now 62, she's 58.

On the last evening of our visit I went alone to the sea. My reverie was disturbed by the murmur of voices. Ah, it was the noise of the waves; they were talking among themselves as they rose and fell under a moonless night in the Bay of Bengal. Suddenly, a swimmer appeared out of the darkness and swam ashore. It was one of us. It was Bill Weipers (later, Sir William), the Dean of the Glasgow Veterinary College. We had much to discuss.

This ancient civilization had much to teach us but the poverty of India would hold back our professional colleagues for a long time. Their intellectual capacity gave us the hope that we could find the means for young veterinary educators to profit from graduate study in the West. Our visit had made it possible for this to occur.

Leaving Madras, we went northward to the state of Andhra Pradesh. The Nisam of Hyderabad had endowed a university there and we stayed at a hostel converted from the residence of one of his princes. We were welcomed at lunch by veterinary students. I sat next to a loquacious young man who spoke with the traditional Bombay-Welsh accent. He enquired: "Sir, do you teach psychology at your veterinary college?" I replied, "Not as a subject on the curriculum." I followed up saying that some abnormalities in pets are improved by psychological therapy undertaken by their owners. "No, no, Sir, I don't mean that. I will give details of a recent case at our clinic." A dog had been run over by a rickshaw, resulting in a compound fracture of the femur. After setting the bone and applying a cast, therapy had included the use of a rickshaw, passed over the affected area daily, with the expectation that the dog would avoid a recurrence. We went on to something else when I said it couldn't happen in Canada because we have no rickshaws.

At the end of the luncheon there was an opportunity for a discussion of student problems. Their spokesperson summed up what had been decided they should ask - "Are you going to recommend that scholarships be offered to underwrite fees and all other expenses for a degree course in veterinary medicine?" Our spokesperson replied that we had come with an open mind and we wished them well.

Following a few days assessing the veterinary program at Hyderabad we went on to the west coast to visit the Bombay Veterinary College at Parel, on the outskirts of the city. We stayed at a hotel in the city and carried a hard boiled egg in a box lunch daily. On one occasion my egg contained a well developed embryo chick!

Bombay was a "dry" town. Nothing makes one feel more like a dipsomaniac than the ritual to obtain a permit from Indian bureaucrats and then to join others showing their permits to enter a locked enclave in the hotel, for a social drink of Scotch whisky!

A two-week seminar on veterinary education was held in Bombay when the seven members of the mission joined 60 Asians, from India, Malaya, Sri Lanka, Pakistan and Afghanistan. When they were a part of the British Empire, these countries were served by a nucleus of officers of the British Colonial Veterinary Service, but as each became politically independent, they have struggled to provide their own.

The mission held general discussions about the recommendations that would be appropriate to include in our report. Informally we ranged far more widely than our particular mandate. Clear to all of us was the fact that poverty was the main handicap to the pace of improvement. But for us we enjoyed the manifold delights of India; the beautiful mosques and palaces, built, albeit with slave labour, yet achieved millennia before the technical revolution. So often the people we met socially expressed a natural talent to engage in conversation, with insight, on 'just about any subject'.

Indians have an appetite for oratory. Free-ranging political theories, including communism, arise at almost any social opportunity. This is particularly irritating to visitors from the United States but I think it is fair to say that this tendency gives a clue to the facility Indians show in finding the social sciences so much easier than other aspects of education. In any case, intellectual training is difficult and can be painful. What is easier is to memorise without necessarily reaching the stage of thinking. Mission members felt that veterinary students they met in India seem to have fallen into a trap of wanting to anticipate answers to questions on examinations rather than learning principles that endure. It is thought to be unfair to students for them to be able to say, "But, Sir, my notes give me no answer to your question six!"

After being in India for a short while, the poverty, though pervasive, does not seem to retain its effect. My eyes developed an impermeable glaze. I no longer seemed to react to the deprivation. But, in retrospect, the comparison between the orderly life of my home country and the city streets of India is still vivid in my memory.

To be born in poverty is a cruel accident and it requires public effort and public funds to improve standards of education, health and all other levels, involved in overcoming this handicap. We resolved individually to exercise our influence in effecting arrangements for faculty members in Indian veterinary colleges to gain financial support for upgrading their education through graduate study at several of the universities represented by the mission.

14
SOUTH AMERICA

The Pan-American Sanitary Bureau is a part of the World Health Organization of the United Nations. Its mandate is broad enough to cover aspects of public health which are dealt with by the veterinary profession. These include control programs of diseases common to animals and humans, and in particular regulations to preserve the wholesomeness and safety of meat and milk products, for human consumption.

In 1959 I was appointed an education consultant for the Bureau. This assignment required me to visit several veterinary schools and institutions which had some association with veterinary education in South America - and a veterinary college in Mexico City.

Some time before I was due to leave I wrote to Hon. Sidney Smith, who had left the president's chair at the University of Toronto to become Minister of External Affairs in the Diefenbaker government. I gave him my itinerary. A long telegram came in reply to say that embassies at Mexico City, Lima, Peru, Santiago, Chile, Buenos Aires, Argentina and Rio de Janeiro had been notified of the dates when I was due at those locations. This was very helpful to fulfilling my assignments. Transportation was supplied where needed and the hospitality of embassy staff and their wives was a great comfort at the end of long days of interviews through interpreters. Occasionally, staff members would accompany me on interviews. Canadians are well received in all the countries I visited.

The specific recommendations in my report remain the property of the U.N. agency I represented. It can be said however that the education in general in the field I represented seemed highly theoretical, as though the memory rather than the mind had been the process used in the classroom. Leaders require a richer diet than this, to deal with problems that arise for professional consideration and solution.

In all of the veterinary colleges visited most of the teachers were part-time. Many for example spent no more than two hours per week to present lectures. Little or no research was being done, while clinical training occupied relatively few hours of a student's time. These two activities are essential to a vibrant teaching program.

Teachers on the veterinary faculty in a few instances came from research institutes, and some were operating private veterinary practices. These sources add to their qualifications but the common practise is for the majority of teachers to be hired on a part-time basis. This makes it difficult to develop a sense of commitment and loyalty to the college.

The physical assets of an education institution are easier to assess than the quality of the teaching staff. In dealing with the latter it is helpful to review both the research and the clinical training program. If both of these are of good quality there is reason to assume that the teachers are competent. In the 8 veterinary colleges I visited in South America there was a considerable variation in both of these features and none met the standards I was used to in North America and Europe.

Language problems were dealt with very satisfactorily both for Portuguese in Brazil and for Spanish in the rest. Most interpreters were university professors. My interpreter in Buenos Aires was a professor of physics. He was fluent in English, with a mother-country accent. He was an excellent interpreter and he showed the manner of a gentleman, which I venture to describe as an unsought self-worth, a sure sign of good breeding. Imagine my surprise at the time he was due to leave and - having detected that I was Welsh - he said, "Well, Cymri am byth, eh?" (Wales for ever) and, "Down with the English; goodbye!"

It was a surprise for me to witness the advance planning occurring in Lima, Peru, where the old and inadequate facilities were being replaced by a new building, with new equipment. The Dean, Teodoro Ramos Saco, had travelled widely in search of ideas when a decision had been made for the building of a modern school of veterinary medicine. Judicious use of capital grants and fellowships from various sources were evident for support of teaching and research. This new school is not as large as some I saw in South America but it was rapidly becoming an outstanding one. The dean has organized the faculty personnel into departments, which will facilitate the development of a sound education program.

Before beginning this assignment in South America I was told to assess and make recommendations for strengthening the teaching of veterinary public health, but I was not to confine myself to this subject. Accordingly, my report was directed not only to the 8 veterinary colleges I visited but also to the sources of financial support of all of these institutions. A separate appendix was added for each of the colleges, detailing strengths and weaknesses of each. In general, there was a need to improve the management skills of senior administrative staff and to develop a full-time commitment to both teaching and research by most members of faculty. The public interest is enhanced by a program of veterinary education of good quality.

The livestock industry is very important in the economy of South America. Much of this includes export trade in meat and meat products. The veterinary component in support of this industry would be improved by achieving higher standards in the education of veterinarians, particularly in placing greater emphasis on the clinical training program. The resources and infrastructure for pasture-fed meat-producing animals is available in most of these countries and should be put to greater use in today's burgeoning global economy. Countries needing to import meat and meat products will always be vigilant about the safety and wholesomeness of the food they import.

My final comment on the visit to South America is to mention the Anglo-Argentines. In Argentina I spent most of my time in Buenos Aires and nearby Azul, but I also went to La Plata and to the northern city of Corrientes, where the Dorado Club is close by. This is an angler's club, established in 1937 by the English on the north bank of the Parana River. Further evidence of the British connection in Argentina is highly visible throughout the countryside by the railway stations, which are very much a look-alike of those in Britain. The whole rail system was built by British contractors. British clubs are found in several locations; the Albion in Buenos Aires was founded in 1893 and changed its name to the English Club in 1898.

Business men and women of the Anglo-Argentine community are still relied upon for their honesty. They tend to ignore the corrupt politics of the state government. Even after the Falklands-Malvinas war in the early 80's they are still regarded as being more reliable than alternative nationals occupying positions of power. The Anglos seem to have bypassed politics. Indeed, British investors are setting up all over the country. Expatriates reveal this phenomenon for a casual visitor to notice, and the news from Argentina, within two decades of a fierce war, is showing that Anglo-Argentines and their issue can survive the ancient dictatorship of the Conquistadores.

15

Sudan and Kenya

In 1963 I was the leader of a Mission for the Food and Agriculture Organization of the U.N., to the University of Khartoum, Sudan. Sir Thomas Dalling, a staff member of F.A.O. in Rome, and Dr. H.C. Adler, a Swiss veterinarian, were the other team members. The purpose of the Mission was to study and assess the education potential of the Faculty of Veterinary Science and to explore ways and means of obtaining the full utilization of the existing facilities. The university was considering the possibility of developing a regional compact whereby applications for entrance would be accepted from nationals in countries contiguous to Sudan. There was in place an informal arrangement accepting foreign students up to ten per cent of the student body. The proposed compact would require per capita grants from participating governments. Such a policy makes sense, particularly for professional degree courses to be available on a regional basis, where English is spoken as a common language in the region. One of the important advantages of this, especially in the relatively new independent countries in Africa, is that it promotes regional cooperation.

Another development that required advice from the Mission was the State plan for an expansion of livestock production to meet the needs of an increase in the population and an anticipated rise in living standards. Our discussions required us to estimate the needs for an increase in veterinary resources to deal with this plan of expansion. The necessary changes dealt with the quality of the education and research programs as well as the size of the manpower requirement. Important in this was the assistance that could be anticipated from the report of the Mission, through the influence of the F.A.O. of the U.N.

After some days of intensive work on the business of the Mission in very hot, humid weather, I was pleased to hear Sir Thomas say, "Saturday is a free day for us. I want to take you to the ancient city of Omderman."

Here we saw a few aboriginals from Southern Sudan, the Nilotes who, at home, are not at all hampered by dress! Having come to the North, where civilizing influences have existed for four centuries, they wore a simple piece of sackcloth.

The division of Sudan into northern and southern regions is an example of the age old problem of North Africa into Arabism and Negritude (black Africa), with their rival claims. In Sudan there is a lopsided advantage for the north which leaves it with the power to keep its Southern nationals subservient.

The Nilotes live in a swamp-girt fen, and time for them stood still for centuries, while around them a more favourable environment allowed the people in some degree to prosper. The heathen Nilotes in the south are no match for Islamic influences in the north. Modern technology is making rapid strides towards improving human welfare but a lot depends on the attitude of the Sudanese in the north in solving age old problems with their countrymen in the south. These were the problems Sir Thomas and I discussed on our free day in Omderman.

When the Mission in Khartoum came to an end we flew to Nairobi. Our Mission here was to visit the University of East Africa to assess the Faculty of Veterinary Science located a few miles away at Kabete.

The University of East Africa has been an interesting experiment in international cooperation which is very important in the development of emerging autonomous countries in Africa. The Faculty at Kabete has been very fortunate to receive generous financial support from the Rockerfeller Foundation in New York. This is a good example of international development which requires the goodwill and cooperation from government and private sectors the world over. In this particular case it promotes the idea that provision of professional education can be organized through intergovernment agreement. A good reason for dealing with this subject in this way is to map out where the different professions in a geographic region should be placed, and to distribute the financial burden in so doing. The case in point is made easier by the fact that English as a second language is common to East African countries and serves as the language of instruction. This factor can apply in most regions in Africa. Rivalry between the emerging governments is the chief obstacle to this policy being used as often as it should be.

As generous as the Rockerfeller Foundation support had been I gained an impression that the job was about half over - that a continuing grant would change the total program from a reasonably good one to a world class example of what a veterinary education program should be in the Kabete setting. I had Sir Thomas Dalling's encouragement to write a Brief giving a detailed account for a plan of expanding graduate studies and training of teachers for a ten year program beginning in 1964. This would have provided 10 visiting professors, for a period of 2 years each, 16 veterinarians, for 2 years, half Africans, selected as potential teaching staff, and 8 non-Africans giving at least 1 year's service as fulltime teachers. Each of the latter group would be graduate students and would serve as demonstrators in laboratory courses to undergraduate students. A Board, with representation from the Rockerfeller Foundation, the Veterinary College and F.A.O. would oversee this plan. My estimate of the cost of this program in 1964 was in the order of $500,000 U.S.

I went to New York to discuss this proposal. Rockerfeller representatives were clearly interested in any effort to strengthen the Kabete program and would like to see an expansion of the plan the Foundation had supported. However, this would have to be financed from other sources because a commitment had been made with the Foundation's grant that further funding from that source should not be expected.

Surprises are common when one is away from home. I was being driven in Kabete by Lars Karstad, an ex-colleague of mine at Guelph. Lars had chosen Kenya as a refuge from a chronic respiratory problem he had suffered in his home environment. He has done very good work with diseases of wild species of animals. I noticed a sign Seago, identifying a resident by that name. I said to Lars, "Among modern English landscape painters my favourite is Edward Seago (1910-1974). I wonder if this is a relative." Lars said, "It's his brother, would you like to meet him?" Here was a charming gentleman who like Lars had chosen Kenya as a refuge. He had suffered from pulmonary tuberculosis and was advised to live in a less humid climate than England.

Over the phone Mr. Seago told Lars he had moved to a new house that day but he still had the fire going in the grate, two chairs and a bottle of wine. "Bring your friends over." We had finished dinner with Lars and his wife and daughter. Lars took my wife Frances and me and we had a pleasant evening. Our host told us where we could see his brother's landscapes at a private gallery in London. We were there the following week and we went to the Marlborough Fine Arts Studio on Abermarle Street.

This pleasant evening with Edward Seago's brother was a highlight of my African adventures. His vocation in Kenya was to arrange consignments of wild animal species to zoos and other establishments. A recent contract involved the movement of living specimens to an island in the Philippines, owned by a wealthy Texan. It happened that Seago met Ferdinand Marcos, the Dictator of the Philippines who was in Nairobi on an international conference and asked for his help in arranging this shipment. Marcos was soon in touch with a shipping magnate of his acquaintance and the deal was satisfactorily completed. Seago's closest friend and assistant was delegated to accompany the shipment and stay long enough to see that the animals were well adapted to their new environment. In the process he had been well looked after by Marcos and was a favourite of his wife Imelda. He fell in love with a beautiful Filipino girl but she was not high in the social order, which displeased Imelda. However, he persisted and they were married in the Dictator's palace!

While visiting London shortly after this, my wife and I viewed masterpieces of Edward Seago's paintings at the Abermarle Street Studio. They were similar in style to the great Constable. Alas! we found the minimum price was in the order of ten thousand pounds sterling.

16

AFGHANISTAN

By 1975 I had become Professor Emeritus at my university. I received a call from Dr. M. Braend of the Food and Agriculture Organization in Rome asking if I was free to be Team Leader of a mission to the University of Kabul, Afghanistan. Other members of the team were Dr. Braend and Dr. A. Neimann-Sorensen of Copenhagen, Denmark.

Our terms of reference included:

1. Study and evaluate the conditions and infrastructure of the livestock industry of Afghanistan.
2. Estimate, on the basis of #1, the immediate and long-term needs for trained animal health and animal production personnel at all levels.
3. Study of the organization of animal production education in the Faculty of Agriculture, and to relate this to the need of the teaching of animal production in the Faculty of Veterinary Science.
4. Prepare a development plan for the Faculty of Veterinary Science, suited to Afghanistan's needs for veterinary manpower.

The mission had been requested by the Ministry of Planning of the State Government through consultation with officials at the Office of the United Nations Development Program in Kabul.

We met with the Ministers and Deputy Ministers of the appropriate departments of the government, and with the Rector of the University and Dean and faculty of Veterinary Science.

Our recommendations were made orally and in a written report after intensive review of physical facilities and discussion with personnel of the broad field of animal health and production.

Without going into details, our recommendations dealt with factors related to a low production output caused by overstocking and over grazing resulting from erosion. Winters are severe and feed reserves are scarce. All of these factors and others account for a low level of nutrition. Inevitably, these conditions render livestock vulnerable to disease. We gave our opinion of the ways the veterinary resources in quality and manpower needed to be improved.

On the day we left Kabul I had asked the dean to arrange a morning session with all the faculty members of the Veterinary College and any other university personnel he thought might be interested.

The morning started with the usual cup of tea. Every day we got used to the concern for our comfort. If we had planned 3 or 4 visits to different areas of the college in one morning, there would be tea laid on at every change, served out of glass cups and saucers.

As team leader I started the session with an expression of thanks for their courtesies, etc., then went on to discuss the strengths and weaknesses of their program, indicating what improvements should be considered to meet Afghanistan's needs in veterinary manpower. Such an exercise is made difficult when everything one says has to go through an interpreter. I believe our interpreter had spent two years in the U.S. and he had been learning English at home in preparation for this trip. But the Afghans are very loquacious and as soon as the interpreter tells them what was said, a long chatter session ensues! It is impossible to tell what level of understanding has transpired. Mission members soldiered on with this session while the temperature rose to a point of discomfort.

Towards the end of the session one of our group whispered to the dean who pressed a button and in came a flunky. This worthy took a key from the dean's desk and came up with a roll of toilet paper. On returning from the washroom, the roll was replaced. Later, I had the same urge and when the flunky took me into the corridor, two underflunkies took me to the washroom, armed with the roll. There is no end to surprises when one is away from home.

Since my visit to Afghanistan the Russian Army has penetrated the Hindu Kush from the north with a devastating effect on the ever-present instability of this country, but without being able to claim a conquest. They left behind a civil war that has shown little sign of prospects for peace. But before ending my experiences in this fascinating part of the world I will give an account of some differences to be seen by a Canadian spending a short visit in a culture so removed from his own.

A sign of the times is seen where the new Khyber Pass, built by the U.S. during World War II, passes the old Khyber. The signpost directs the traffic so that "buses" go on the new and "camels" on the old!

The free spirit in all of us is the normal life-style experience for the majority of people in Afghanistan. It has been called a nation of brigands and this because of the prevalent freebooting nomadic existence of the sheep and goat owners. An illiteracy rate of 90 percent (98 percent among the women) among a population of 15 million is compensated for by the delightful freedom that comes with a migratory or transhumant system which is the dominating feature of the Afghan sheep industry.

There are upwards of 24 million sheep and 3.5 million goats, of which 80 percent migrate in varying degrees every year. In some areas the flock may travel only two or three days but many are driven for two months to mountain grazing areas for the summer, staying two months there and spending two months on the return journey to their winter grazing area. The spring migration begins in April and ends in October. Very little all-year-round grazing occurs in Afghanistan because of the low rainfall.

Imagine yourself travelling with the Kuchi band that treks 1000 miles a year. This involves something like 100 nomads with 50 camels, 12 donkeys, 5 horses and 600 sheep, moving from Nawar, the winter headquarters, to Garmsel, which means "warm valley". When it's time to move on, the cameleers load their kneeling, protesting animals, groaning with displeasure under sacks of straw, skins of oil and water, carpets for sale, mattocks and blackened pots, topped with babies wrapped like mummies lashed to the loads.

Apart from the Karakul, the sheep are of the fat-tail variety, so-called because of the development of two fat-containing pouches on either side of the tail, which enlarge as winter approaches. The sheep use this nutritive source as a means of survival under the severe environmental conditions when the term zero grazing means no grazing at all. Looking at the fat-tails in December as they trot away reminds one of the rear view of waddling fat women.

The famous Karakul sheep, from which pelts of the newborn lamb are used for coats, caps and hats, numbering some seven million, are all found in the north - north of the Hindu Kush, a range of mountains running east and west. This range provides a natural barricade between the Russian influence which shares its northern border and all the other influences - Iran to the west, China to the east, the subcontinent of India to the east and south. The Afghans have been the keepers of the crossroads for not only neighbouring states but for the invaders of long centuries; Alexander the Great, the Mongol hordes of Genghis Khan and Tamerlane, of the Arabs, and more recently, the British. Today's invaders are represented by most of the nations of the world proffering aid through international development projects. The United States and Russia have provided metal highways, the

Chinese have built hydro-electric and irrigation systems, the Germans and others have constructed educational facilities.

Half a million people in the capital of Kabul give evidence that Afghanistan is an amalgam of many tribes. High black boots and long striped robes are worn by the Uzbecs and Turkomans from the north. The influential Pushtuns wear their knee-length shirts with the tails out, over baggy pantaloons, while the Kabulis wear ordinary western-style clothes and Karakul hats. In contrast, the Tajis wear turbans. Very few women are seen on the streets of this strict, Islamic country. They are denied face and form by being clothed in a chadri, a sleeveless, pleated head-to-toe covering. Old customs are very hard to change in spite of the fact that Afghan law no longer requires the chadri to be worn. Things are changing, though. At the hotel where I stayed I witnessed a Muslim wedding reception where all the guests were wearing clothes that would be normal with us.

The romantic and delightful differences which characterize the simple life in Afghanistan are gradually disappearing. Kabul, like the Khyber, has an old and a new section. The new is modern and so different from Asian cities which, to me, all look the same - Calcutta, Singapore, Teheran, Delhi, Bombay, Rangoon - put me in the middle of any of these and the differences are subtle. Kabul has wide streets and sidewalks, well built highrise government buildings and relatively little traffic.

17
BIHAR AND ASSAM

On my second trip to India, in 1971, I was a member of an appraisal mission of the International Bank for Reconstruction and Development. Its headquarters, as part of the World Bank, are in Washington, D.C.

There has been criticism of the IBRD, mainly from the CATO Institute, a libertarian think-tank in Washington which seems to deliberately misunderstand the purposes of the Bank. The phenomenal growth of the economies of some developing countries, helped by IBRD and other associated financial institutions of the World Bank, is evidence that the primary objectives are being met.

The purpose of the mission was to visit certain professional colleges in the states of Bihar and Assam with the view to linking them administratively with existing universities. Several advantages were thought to accrue from such an arrangement, particularly when a number of colleges and schools occupy a single campus. The so-called agricultural universities that developed from the Land Grant Colleges in the United States served as the basis for our discussions with the authorities and staff of the colleges we visited. Such institutions first began as agricultural colleges with veterinary medicine and household science added. After the second world war most of them became fully-fledged universities.

Many advantages occur in being a part of a university. These include cohabitation with schools and students of a variety of disciplines, including specialists in cognate subjects, e.g. animal science, biochemistry and genetics. There would be a wider range of supervisors and advisors for graduate degree programs.

The social and extracurricular activities on a university campus offer an opportunity for expanding the horizons of young people at a very important period of their development. With this in mind, members of the team were expected to assess the value of such a change and in my case I was to consider the feasibility of establishing one veterinary college in a university setting in each of the states instead of two that existed in both Bihar and Assam.

Agencies offering foreign aid deal with the Central Government in Delhi, to ensure approval by that source is obtained before proceeding with financial assistance for state projects. The mission therefore spent three days in Delhi for discussions of vital concern to us, before the visit to the two states. Members of the mission were impressed with the high calibre of senior civil servants we dealt with in Delhi.

The disciplines represented on the team were Architecture, Household Science, Animal Science, Plant Science and Veterinary Medicine. It was helpful for the team members to meet together each evening to compare notes and share experiences. I had visited the veterinary college in Patna, Bihar in 1953 and found on this second visit that lack of funds prevented the college from implementing many of the recommendations made 18 years previously. It was clear that outside agencies such as the World Bank would be needed to provide the financial support to improve what was offered in educating students for veterinary services in India.

After completing my assignment in Patna and Ranchi, my report to the Bank recommended that the Patna College should be closed and that one state veterinary college should be established by combining the worthwhile assets of the two existing veterinary colleges. I expressed my preference for a relocation of this combination of assets to a university campus but such an outcome would require far more study beyond the scope of the present visit.

Bihar is considered to be the poorest state in India and it seemed understandable that in the four decades that had gone by following its establishment, the Patna College had suffered from financial neglect. The Veterinary College at Ranchi was first occupied in 1962. Again, inadequate financing during the decade of its existence had left the building far from complete. With modest improvements at Ranchi there was good reason to phase-out the Patna College as soon as possible and move some of the staff to Ranchi. This was expected to be an interim move that had its value during the period of planning for the relocation to a new site on the campus of a university. It was clear that any suggestion involving a move from home for these people is a major difficult problem when it becomes a requirement. I believe this is so mainly because having a job and a place to live seems almost always better than taking a chance on a change.

I am reminded here of a discussion I had with graduating veterinary students in Ranchi. After telling them about the purpose of my visit I asked if they had any questions. The young man who appeared to be the leader of the class asked if the World Bank was going to guarantee each of the students a job!

In Assam I went to the veterinary college at Khanapaka, Guahati, with separate buildings at Jorhat, first occupied in 1948. There was a request from college authorities which surprised me. High priority was given for hostel accommodation for 100 farmers to participate in the extension program. Here I was appraising the program of veterinary education and finding many ways to improve it. Clearly I must put first things first, even though I had a deep interest in the desire of the college staff to teach producers of farm livestock, at the same time as their primary task of teaching veterinary students. It reminded me of the days when I was Provincial Animal Pathologist in Alberta. In the winter I would attend meetings in little rural schools for the same purpose and this increased the farmers' knowledge of livestock production.

On probing this subject I discovered that the State Act relating to the college at Guahati specifies that staff members will devote one third of their time to teaching, research and extension, and as for the last mentioned I concluded that the request for sleeping accommodation was as simple as saying "Give us the tools!".

Another source of helpful information for me was a request I made to interview the civil servants who occupied the position of chief veterinary officer in the central government and in the two state governments. I sought their opinion on the idea of joining the veterinary colleges with agricultural universities. None of them approved of the idea, even after I described the advantages that would follow such a move. I was pleased for many of them to say they were visiting lecturers at the veterinary colleges and I urged them to make good use of any assistance they could give in this respect, but the idea of linking with a university had no appeal. It took further prodding for me to find the reason why they resisted this proposal. It wasn't until I discovered that they had been acting as external examiners and this provided very handsome added income for them. The colleges had been following the British system in the matter of external examiners and those who gained personal income from this source came to know that there was no recognition of such a category in North American universities.

In both Bihar and Assam several items arose in assessing the needs of the proposed change in the relocation of the veterinary colleges by linking them with so-called agricultural universities. It was essential for instance to plan an estimate of class size because of the impact this would have on the ratio of staff to students. I discussed the organization of professional staff into departments. An important point here is that heads of departments accept responsibility for staff under them and it reduces the number of people reporting to the dean. We also discussed a program of leave for further education.

It surprises me that India does not seem to use the category of technicians to assist the professional staff. It has a large number of reasonably well-educated unemployed people who could be trained to do chemical and other laboratory tests and to prepare for laboratory sessions, leaving the professional staff more free time to deal with teaching and research for which they are the only ones equipped in both education and experience. Technicians soon learn their job and become better at it than their supervisors, and at less cost.

The friendly welcome and hospitality received on these visits will not be forgotten. I made an unusual request resulting from a discussion with the dean of veterinary medicine at Ranchi. We had become friends on my first visit to India 18 years previously and I ventured to enquire about the caste system which divides Hindu Society into four major hereditary classes, each being separated from the others in occupation and marriage. Legislation has given some support for the lower castes but I asked him if the lowest of the major Hindu castes, the Sudra, were seen locally. Originally, these were the menials who have become artisans and labourers. "Yes," he said, "I will arrange for a car to take you tomorrow to a valley close by and I shall be pleased to accompany you." Bless him, I did not know how he would take my request but I am pleased to say that I had this experience of being in a community in a part of the world where people did not use money. Their main item for barter was jute, handmade into rope, cordage or sacking. They carried their product to the road above the valley and bartered for items needed in their simple existence. I noticed several faces with pock-marked eruptions, showing that smallpox was endemic in the valley. Mothers nursed their babies with absolutely no sense of shame. They were a smiling people and they seemed happy. Poverty is a much harsher thing to see when one is walking the streets of Calcutta.

In Assam I had been told that the best herd of Jersey cattle in India was owned and operated by the airport from which planes were crossing the nearby border, in the war with China. One of the senior airport personnel happened to have completed a degree course in agriculture and he had noticed the large area of land suitable for growing alfalfa and grasses suitable for supporting a cow herd, by zero grazing.

I had lunch with this air force officer at the airport mess and heard his fascinating story in achieving this ambitious program. He had much to tell me of the community interest in support of this development and I was taken to see the herd, and this delayed our lunch. My plane was due to leave in half an hour but I was told not to worry. My host said, "I have told the pilot you will be on this flight," but there were no signs of a meal! When I was finally taken to the plane the pilot and his staff were in line to shake my hand and welcome me aboard! As soon as the engines were ready for take-off, they were throttled down, the door was opened and someone came aboard to offer me a gift - 2 lbs of Assam tea.

Before finishing this chapter I want to recall my experience the last day in Assam. It is not to be forgotten. I felt miserable with the third day of a bad cold when members of the mission were told, "Tomorrow is an opportunity for you to take an elephant ride to see white rhinos in their natural habitat". I was not to be deterred! At 4.30 A.M. I had a wake-up call for a 5 A.M. elephant ride. There were 3 of them, with space for 3 of us on each.

Farm Transport in Assam.

On approaching the elephant I was assigned to, I noticed the owner unrolling a piece of cloth from which the elephant's 2 tusks rolled out. He proceeded to screw them on to the roots of the tusks. He said, "I put them under my pillow every night. I can't take a chance of them being sawn off and sold for ivory." To get to our seats we climbed steps to the level of the elephant's back then slid into one of the seats which had a rope to clutch with our hands for safety. On command the elephant started plodding towards the open savannah, eventually heading for a lake. I thought this was to give the giant beasts their morning drink. Instead, they plodded into the lake, to the other side.

At last, a rhino was sighted and forgetting my cold, I felt like a very privileged sightseer - then another one appeared, and another - elephants and rhinos before 8 o'clock in the morning! In comparison, the return journey was uneventful excepting for our chatter on the good fortune of being where we were.

After thanking our hosts for their hospitality we headed for the Dum Dum airport on the outskirts of Calcutta after a busy period of work, followed by an unusual ending.

18
PHILIPPINES

My wife Frances and I lived in an apartment in Makati, the favoured district in Manila, from February 21, 1978 to April 29, 1978. The request for my services as a consultant was for a period of 6 months but by mid-April I told Dr. Augusto L. Tenmatay, to whom I was responsible, that I was ready to write my report. I thought I would not be showing a sense of responsibility by staying on. My report would not have been significantly improved and the expense I felt could not be justified for me to stay out the 6 months as tempting as this happy experience was proving to be.

The project proposal was financed by an educational loan from the World Bank, under the jurisdiction of the Educational Development Projects Implementing Task Force! (EDPITAF) of the Department of Education and Culture.

The government had proposed that the veterinary college, University of the Philippines, located on the outskirts of Metro Manila, at Diliman, should be relocated to Los Banôs, about 40 miles away. The government report expressed the expectation that the relocated college would become a national resource of excellence for veterinary education, research and extension. Imagine my delight in having to consider all the features required to make this a reality!

It was necessary for me to assess the existing plant and estimate the requirements of all categories of personnel, equipment, the classrooms, offices, laboratories and all other physical resources. Basic to all of these was the estimation of an annual intake of students per year and an expansion of the research programs.

I had good cooperation from the professional staff and with the odd exception of those having personal reasons for not wanting to move, the majority were enthusiastic when they understood the commitment of financial support and pride over the claim that the new college would become a national asset. Veterinary education had never before been a spotlight item in the Philippines.

I worked hard in tropical heat for two months to obtain the information needed for my purpose. After my report was read by Dr. Tenmatay and Dr. Perfecto, I received an invitation for Frances and me to be their guests for lunch.

Cattle ranch in Mindenao, Philippines.

Let me digress to introduce Dr. Perfecto. He was my correspondent for about two years of negotiations about the project. Initially, I was asked to spend two years in developing what was no more than an idea arising from discussions within EDPITAF, of which Dr. Perfecto was then the head. I was unwilling to spend two years of my valuable time in retirement but he kept writing and eventually it was agreed that preliminary work would be done locally if a financial commitment was made for relocation plans to be effected. At that stage I agreed to spend 6 months in working on a complete feasibility report and I asked if my wife would be allowed to accompany me.

Imagine our surprise when we arrived to be told that Dr. Perfecto was a candidate at an election called by the dictator, Ferdinand Marcos. Perfecto was on the Marcos ticket and he won, having the lowest number of votes in Metro-Manila among those elected.

The candidate who failed to win election through having just a few less votes than Perfecto was Benigno Aquino who campaigned from jail. He was assassinated 8 years later by Marcos forces and his wife Corazon Aquino ultimately became president when Marcos fled the country to exile in Hawaii.

On the day of the luncheon Frances and I went to EDPITAF headquarters and met Dr. Tenmatay and Dr. Perfecto. Two cars were laid on to take us to the restaurant. Perfecto knew how vulnerable he was over assassination attempts on him by supporters of Aquino. Perfecto's removal from the scene would automatically allow Aquino, by the votes he obtained, to be elected in his stead. Perfecto said to me, "You and your wife will ride with Dr. Tenmatay. My bodyguard will drive me. I don't want you two to suffer an accident, so close to your departure date!".

When we settled in at the restaurant we were told this was the first time they had taken a consultant to lunch to celebrate after receiving a report and they presented me with a brass Plaque of Appreciation - "To All Men to Whom These Presents May Come, Greetings", etc.

I suppose consultants can't expect an organization as complex as the World Bank or a UN Agency to keep in touch with them over the outcome of a consultancy. I have never received feedback after returning from a trip. I did however receive a visit from the associate dean at Diliman who came to Guelph some years after I had returned from the University of the Philippines. He told me that all my recommendations had been accepted and were acted upon. This was reassuring but seemed too good to be true. He had no evidence on paper to support his comment, and did not seem to have a desire to discuss the details excepting to say that everything was going well at Los Banôs.

My recommendations were given in eleven categories:

1. Curriculum. I had prepared a table showing average percentage allocation of time for each subject proposed or in use in the following places: old and new at University of the Philippines, Aranata (Philippines), Malaysia, U.S.A. (average), Canada (Guelph and Saskatoon), and Glasgow. Differences ranged no more than 2 percentage points excepting in clinics and zootechnics and these were justified by the former being emphasized in temperate zones while the latter required more emphasis in the tropics because, in both cases, they reflected on the differences in the use of veterinary manpower.

2. Student enrolment - re quota for number to enrol in first year. This was needed to establish a desirable teacher/student ratio and other factors.

3. Facilities and equipment, laboratory space and space for clinics and animal holding areas, classrooms, and research labs. At Los Banôs these were to be used in common with students in animal science. Assessment was required of existing facilities already available for use by veterinary students.

4. Faculty manpower. University of the Philippines regards a ratio of 1:10 faculty/students as satisfactory. This may be reasonable as a target for the entire university but it should take into account that law students for instance in exercises dealing with case-law require a large number to be effective whereas surgical exercises in human and veterinary medicine learn best on a 1 to 1 basis. My recommendation for the overall ratio for veterinary medicine in Los Banôs was no higher than 1:7 which would allow some time for research.

5. Administrative Organization. I recommended there should be 4 departments under the dean: (i) Anatomy and physiology, (ii) Pathology and microbiology, (iii) Medicine and surgery, and (iv) Extension and research. The head of the last mentioned would be more of a coordinator than department head. The others would have section heads for cognate subjects. This set up tends to encourage responsibility from the bottom upwards. At Diliman there seemed to be too many faculty members reporting to the dean, requiring him to make routine decisions that could be reduced to rules. He needed to be free to make important decisions for the welfare of his college.

6. Technical Assistance Component. Apart from improving the business methods in administration, this component would be chosen among foreign experts, and it is of extreme importance to use their influence during the early stage of relocating the college.

7. Graduate Studies. The M.Sc. program should continue as it is but the Ph.D. degree should await adequate resources of supervising faculty to be available.

8. Interface of veterinary medicine and animal science. An important outcome of the project-proposal is the effective cooperation of these two elements in designing programs that will exploit the expertise of each in achieving a livestock program to meet an increase in the number of people who consume meat, milk and poultry products.

9. Research Programs. The college will inherit two locations for its expanded research and extension programs. Diliman will convert its facilities to accommodate the extension program and, mainly, applied research. Los Banôs, with its broad faculty resource, will be engaged mainly in basic research. This will be coordinated with research by animal scientists.

10. Veterinary extension. A section head in the Department of Research and Extension is recommended as a coordinator of services to the public, in both Los Banôs and Diliman but regarding Los Banôs as

his headquarters. He is also to be responsible for organizing the continuing education program for upgrading faculty and technical staff. The latter include sub-professional workers in the field and laboratory assistants. The World Health Organization of the UN defines these categories as "A technical worker in a particular field with less than full qualifications".

I have dwelt on my recommendations as a way of recording a glimpse of the details a consultant finds himself involved in.

This visit to the Philippines was very pleasant. Frances and I enjoyed our cosy apartment at Charter House. There was a park close by where dog shows were held and a pet show that included a baby kangaroo and a chimpanzee! One day Frances was invited by strangers to share their alfresco lunch.

At the zoo we were the only white haired, fair skinned, blue eyed animals there, and we were a source of amusement for the children who paid more attention to us than to the chimpanzees!

The lady at EDPITAF who did my typing, arranged my transportation etc. insisted that we spend a weekend as guests of her father in a nearby barrio. The highlight was to be a Sunday afternoon cock-fight. He showed us the beautiful cock he had chosen for this and he failed to understand why we declined to go to this special entertainment.

We slept on a bamboo bed, too narrow to lie other than to try sleeping so that our feet were level with each other's head!

I brought home several colourful Tagalog shirts, very inexpensive. These are worn outside the trousers and typical wear of the best dressed Filipinos. I also had trousers custom-made at the equivalent of $15 a pair.

In many respects, Manila is the jewel of southeast Asia. It is a modern city with several first class hotels and restaurants. The cultural centre offers entertainment of high quality.

Fidel Ramos took over the government in 1992 after the gap of 6 years from Marcos' time, filled in by Corazon Aquino. In his six years Ramos introduced the basis for a democratic government and turned the ailing economy around. It is too early to see how well his successor will maintain his predecessor's achievements. "Erap", the nickname of Joseph Estrada, took over in May 1998. He is a well known actor and claims to know little about economics but he expected to attract experts to his cabinet to advise him and make up for his deficiencies.

19
NICARAGUA

The three words "Save The Children" identifies an international movement which began in Britain in 1920 to assist the 13 million orphans in Europe after the first world war. It was motivated "to protect child life wherever menaced, regardless of race, creed or nationality, and to help raise the standard of child welfare throughout the world".

José Garcia-Lozano, the Country Director for Canadian Save the Children Fund in Nicaragua, had become acquainted with 2 Jesuit priests who operated the Father Francisco Luis Espinosa Agricultural and Livestock School, 15 miles north of Esteli. The school was named after the one-time director who was killed by the Somosa forces. The school operates a 3 year program in two specialties: "agronomia" (crops) and "zootechnia" (livestock) and had been given a mandate to offer a program of education combining animal production and animal health. The priests were requesting financial and technical assistance in carrying out this mandate, and their request was being supported by José. Cansave (as it came to be called) asked me if I was interested in visiting Esteli to assess the feasibility of this request as a project. The Board was satisfied that José's description of the government's concern about agrarian reform was essential in making food more available for children, particularly the rural poor. Shortly after the Sandinista/Somosa war ended the government began a "food first" program.

Accordingly, I visited Nicaragua from January 27 to February 8, 1984 to carry out my mission. The Sandinistas took over the government in 1979. Over 40,000 landless campesinos (rural poor) were given land instead of being the slaves of Somosa, producing sugar, bananas and other products for export, never having had land to produce food for themselves.

Groups of campesinos were formed into co-operatives, to be eligible for land and credit and their cry was, "show us how". In Esteli, the priests and teachers were training young people to help show them how.

Katrine Van't Hooft was a Spanish speaking, Dutch veterinarian who acted as my language interpreter. She was paid by the Dutch government to work with the campesino farming co-ops around Esteli. She took me to several co-ops and I saw at first hand how important her role was in supplying veterinary service.

I lived as the guest of the priests, who prepared breakfast at their prefab cottage, to the sound of classical music by c.d. We shared beans and rice with the students for the other meals.

The chairman of the Council for Superior Education wanted me to know that his Council was at arms-length to government and that it was the will of government to keep politics out of education. He assured me that I was welcomed by the Council in carrying out my mandate and that my report would be given serious consideration. He explained that Esteli was being run as a private school but that it was under the supervision of his Council.

After discussions with the staff at Esteli, I prepared an outline of a curriculum for a course combining animal production and animal health, with emphasis on practical training, and I estimated the requirement for teachers and other aspects in beginning this new program. An ambulatory clinic would be necessary, to operate at Esteli on animals brought there, and by taking students to co-operatives where they would get "hands on" experience under professional supervision. The supervisor would keep in mind that his students should be trained as advisors to help improve the campesinos as livestock producers.

Katrine Van't Hooft told me that the veterinary college at Utrecht, Holland had more students qualifying than there were jobs available. I took advantage during a European holiday to interview several candidates who were eager for a challenge in Nicaragua. The limit here was the availability of funds for Cansave's support. The upshot was that I hired 2 Dutch veterinarians for a commitment of 2 years. Katrine was willing to come back after completing all requirements and graduating from Utrecht. The other was Hans Rooijakkers. Hans arrived early at Esteli to learn Spanish from a young lady. She found him to be a good pupil and like most Europeans he found it easy to learn Spanish. But wait, this part of my story ends with romance. Teacher and pupil fell in love and were married!

It was fortunate that the Sandinista government chose rural co-operatives as the means of improving the food supply. The expected alternative in a Communist country would have been a state operated program like the one that failed in Russia. But it must be said in retrospect that the Sandinistas would have been more successful in feeding the rural poor if they had emphasized their policy of distributing all the land, taken from the Somosa regime instead of operating so much of it on the basis of State farms in a government plan. Apparently, a free market has a power that cannot be ignored.

From Esteli I was taken to the Cairo Co-operative located close to the border of Honduras. We lost our way and came across an area, ransacked by the Contras during the night. Most of the food and anything else worthwhile had been taken. I put my head into a canvas tent and was pleased to come across a carton of paper bags containing flour, with the sender's name on the outside - a charitable organization in Edmonton, and another which did not reveal its contents, from Owen Sound, Ontario. Eventually, we arrived at the Cairo Co-op where there were 15 men and 3 women serving as directors. The youngest was a 15 year old boy. The leader, with a 47 rifle slung on his shoulder, José Cerrea-Lagos, explained that the community plans to relocate to a site that will provide flat land between their living quarters and the mountains as a means of giving greater protection from ambush and attack by the Contras who came from the intervales of Honduras across the boundary into Nicaragua. The Co-op intended to farm the same land but will build a new barrio.

As they discussed their plans I felt I was listening to a prescription for a Community Centre which is an idea so close to Cansave's ways of improving rural living in poor countries. I found that the directors met every two weeks to review items of supply and production. I asked if the wives were at their meetings - yes, the whole family goes. Did they tend to have a social time after the meetings; yes, they sing and enjoy each other's company. Did this happen in the old regime? No, they were very much on their own and without the means to grow their own food.

On my return to Toronto the Board of Cansave accepted my report which included (1) a training program for technicians in animal production and health, (2) provision of a veterinary service for the campesino co-operatives, and (3) establishment of a veterinary diagnostic laboratory.

I went back to Esteli in 1985 to monitor the progress. By this time the staff member for Cansave in Nicaragua was Joe Gunn known to the Latinos as Pepe Pistole! There were beginnings of a physical expansion to accommodate the new program, but with tales of serious problems over a shortage of construction workers and materials. It was clear that the Sandinistas had become Orthodox Marxists, subordinating needs of the market to central planning and the latter had proved inappropriate. Their first impulse was to raise wages and control prices to the extent that no kind of enterprise found it possible to make a profit. Serious shortages and a burgeoning black market was the result.

I went again from June 19 to July 1, 1989. The Sandinistas had seized power 10 years earlier but were just one year from defeat in their 1990 election. Paul Knox in the *Globe and Mail* puts it this way: "They slew many dragons during those 11 years, but one defeated them: the challenge of creating a coherent, consistent economy policy tailored to a poor, rural Central American Nation."

This (1989) was my third and last visit to Nicaragua. On August 8, 1989 the first class of 17 students graduated from the education program I helped establish in 1984. By that time Cansave had canvassed its supporters for a scholarship fund - the Trevor Lloyd Jones Scholarship at Esteli. The first recipient was Blanca Olivas, who left home at 5 a.m. from Palacaguina, 3 hours away from Esteli. In spite of having epilepsy, Blanca came first in her class.

When this scholarship program began it operated as a subsidy for all students in the program passing successfully from one year to the next. Inflation caused it to be reduced to supporting the first 15 in the class.

Memories of my participation in International Development have probably given more detail than is usual for a biography but I am concerned about the general apathy among the public over attempts to improve the lot of the world's poor people. A global strategy on their behalf should appeal to anyone with a social conscience.

This is being written ten years after an accord, signed in February 1989 by presidents of the countries in Central America, which brought to an end the U.S. sponsored Contra war against Nicaragua. Even Honduras and El Salvador, the 2 surviving client states of the U.S., signed the accord. This surely is evidence that the U.S. capacity to impose its will on independent nations by the use of force is eroding. But Nicaragua had lost 50,000 of its people. The country was bankrupt. Through international development, hope can be brought to where there is none in a crisis like this.

20
TEACHERS

We enter the new millenium with more excellent facilities and well trained teachers, compared with my student days at Guelph. But during the period 1930-34 when I was an undergraduate, we had four outstanding, naturally born teachers who made up for much that was lacking during this important period in my life. I want to make brief mention of them here.

At the top of my list is Henry E. Batt, who came to Canada from England to try his hand at farming a quarter section of Saskatchewan prairie. He was discouraged by the state of the economy when he found it was cheaper to use butter as axle grease than buying lubricating oil, and the price of potatoes was less than the cost of production. He chose to pack up. He found himself in Toronto and became a student at O.V.C., eventually becoming a faculty member.

Dr. Henry Ball, my favourite teacher.

He taught zoology, embryology and histology. His blackboard drawings of the different tissue elements are a graphic depiction that have remained with me all these years. I can see him now with his hands and his white coat covered with white, blue and red chalk, from his blackboard art.

He usually had sound advice for us and seemed to know how to introduce college education to a diverse group with varying abilities to begin at this level. He loved poetry and exposed us to it. He helped to calm us down, realizing that our sense of freedom from home gave free-reign to the influence of lust producing hormones.

His father image was just what we needed. This of course was all superimposed on Henry Batt as a good teacher. He introduced me into a lifelong interest in biology. There was a lighter side too and an appearance in dress of a typical professor. In mid-winter one morning he felt his cheek. "It was dark, I was up too early to shave!". For comfort from the cold, his pajama legs showed below his trousers! Dr. Batt had a glass eye, and when asked to comment on Dr. Schofield's request for a binocular microscope Dr. McGilvray's query was, "Henry, do you need one of these microscopes?" The reply was cryptic,

"No, I have no use for one!". From a person who had no guile this showed the arms-length relationship between Batt and Schofield.

Francis William Schofield was the cleverest of the four on my list. He left O.V.C. and went to Korea as a Christian Missionary in 1916 but he became *persona non grata* by the Japanese rulers of that day - he had signed the Declaration of Independence as a representative of the Korean Independence Movement and in 1920 he returned to O.V.C.

I have already mentioned that I have felt privileged in having Dr. Schofield as my supervisor up to the time I became dean. In the experience of this privilege, it was helpful more in teaching me patience working for one who had the misfortune of being a manic depressive. I had great concern for him when he was melancholic. At this stage, he would have had a sleepless night and had considerable difficulty with presenting lectures the next day. But at the other extreme he was a very good teacher.

In his pathology lab periods he was keen on having specimens showing the signs of disease, either preserved in jars or preferably fresh from the slaughter house.

Not only a good teacher, but his fertile mind made him a productive researcher. During his sleepless nights however a brilliant thought would arise which needed attention the next day and the demands he made on anyone assisting him were peppered with inconsistency. This said, I believe he had the most brilliant mind of anyone on the college faculty.

Wilfrid J.R. Fowler taught surgery and he would demonstrate the different sutures on the lapel of his custom-built jacket. He had long experience in the art of surgical technique but he would have been a good teacher in most subjects of which he was knowledgeable.

He became an expert on roaring in the horse. This requires a delicate operation to control a loose vocal cord which interferes with breathing on inspiration, especially at the end of a race, in thoroughbreds. Dr. Fowler went to France and Ireland to operate on roarers.

Enjoying practical jokes, he had beer glasses with small holes at the brim to cause slobbering, and he once made me sit in a chair on which he had hidden a gadget which sounded as though I had made an anti-social noise!

R.A. McIntosh was a self-taught pedagogue who developed methods of presenting his courses that made it a joy to learn his subjects. Each lecture seemed to be the essence of his thoughts since the previous one. He taught medicine, which amounted to a well-prepared description of the diseases of all the farm animals, providing food and raiment for public consumption. In the final year he had prepared a course with the title, Special Therapeutics. In this were the items of importance and methods of curing the diseases encountered by the practicing veterinarian, and he did it with his special skills. When his students were in practice they would refer to their record of his lectures, kept handy in their car.

I have written about these four favourite teachers of my student days. My inward eye finds it easy to remember them in the classroom or lab, but I do not want to exclude any of those who taught me or have served under my supervision in the 37 years of association with O.V.C. during my interesting career in veterinary education.

21
MUSIC

The pace of life changes in old age. One's expectations are much easier met. There is no compulsion to take it all in by stepping out of the car for 10 minutes. When I'm in my old haunts in the country and want to allow my memory free rein to enjoy my days at *Coediog*, for example, I look for my favourite stile, find a comfortable angle and dream for an afternoon! This brings back not only the panorama before me but memories of the people who lived and farmed this land. More of my generation have left the scene than are still living but I'm sure their ancient spirit has survived.

This brings me to the thought that what I have written of times gone by or the good old days has been separated from contemporary events by my move to Canada. It has surprised me as I grow older that these indomitable spirits of the old times have been an almost daily source of pleasure, and memory is such a valuable asset when one is old.

I have lived to witness mass culture dominating society, whether it be religious cults, muchmusic people, and indeed those who boast about their maiming and killing. This is the horizontal society. The traditional hierarchies no longer rule. For good or ill these groups are changing our world. Anything seems possible with this horizontal identity which transcends religion, race and gender.

Old age is not immune to these disturbing societal changes, but retirement allows an alternative. Here I paraphrase John Masefield, the one-time poet laureat: "Best to dwell on the pleasant things". We have far more freedom to indulge in cultural pursuits in old age than is possible during a busy career. The post-luncheon rest, I find, is a time for reflecting on the good times of yesteryear; sometimes this moves on to reverie.

In chapter one I refer to the lusty singing of hymns at Capel Bethel, often improvising into a six-part harmony and repeating the last two lines once or twice through a reluctance to give up the ascending emotion. Apart from my mother's folk singing, it was my first experience with music and this has got me musing over the place of music in my life. Harmony is the next step in singing, enjoying and often being thrilled with the simple tunes in hymn singing. Welsh people seem to pick up singing in harmony without regard to the score. If the hymn has a particularly good tenor part we sing it but another would find us singing bass. Welsh voices are heard the world over, in beautiful harmony, when a burst of favourite hymns, folk or nonsense songs break out at public gatherings, especially at football and soccer games.

When I came to Canada I joined the choir at St. George's Church, Guelph and the director, Ralph Kidd, put me in the tenor section.

In my student days I went with my lady friend, Gertrude Sorby, to the Presto Music Club concerts and on two occasions we had the great pleasure of hearing the voice of Guelph-born Edward Johnson. He brought delight to his home turf and the experience of several years as a leading tenor of the Metropolitan Opera. About 25 years later, after Edward Johnson had retired to Guelph, I met him and spent a happy day with him. Both of us had been a firm friend of Archdeacon Scovil, the revered rector of St. George's Anglican Church in Guelph. By this time he and his wife had retired and were living in Grimsby. Martin Barry, an agent for the Imperial Insurance Company, was our driver.

The Archdeacon and Mrs. Scovil were delightful hosts for tea. Edward Johnson was a choirboy at St. George's and he was full of his early experiences as a boy in Guelph. That afternoon with but few proddings from us he became the entertainer. He had many stories to relate, including the heartbreaks. He found it was hard for a Canadian, no matter how well-trained, to compete with European imports in the world of opera. At one stage he Italianized his name to Edoardo di Geovanni!

That afternoon went quickly but on the way home our conversation became serious. Edward Johnson reminded Martin and me of his attempts to promote music in the Guelph schools, where some years ago he had given $25,000 to the school boards to support a music program. Martin chimed in and said, "I've suggested to Edward that the Rotary Club might be a good agency to advance the ideas that are going through his mind."

At the next Rotary meeting Martin said to me, "I'd like you and Jim Schroder to drop in at my house at 4 this afternoon." He had been talking to Edward the day before about changes in his will. If Rotary was willing to establish an independent Foundation for the funding of music programs in Guelph, he would provide substantial support in his will as a reasonable guarantee that such a project would be successful.

An *ad hoc* committee of Rotary convinced the Board to approve a new project, to establish the Edward Johnson Music Foundation. A charter was drafted, dated November 29, 1957. I was appointed the first president, and the first board of directors were all Rotarians, being the facilitators. Soon the Foundation became well established as a new independent organization to promote music in Guelph.

We organized a mailing campaign for donations in 1958. In preparing the brochure I mentioned "We feel that a community's cultural growth should keep pace with its industrial expansion". We were disappointed with our first attempt when we raised only $2000. But, from 1959 to 1963, many violin students were given free instruction at elementary and intermediate levels. At great sacrifice of her time and talent, Jessie Lamb, bless her soul, nurtured her pupils through the trying period of scratchings, to sound notes on those strings.

Lack of funds prevented any significant development for some years after the Foundation was formed except for the "crusade for strings" which began in 1956 with Edward Johnson donating $1700 to pay for the lessons. Beginners were given class instruction, while any that had previous experience were given private lessons.

Edward Johnson died suddenly on December 11, 1959. I was entering the funeral home when his daughter Fiorenza and her husband George Drew were leaving. I offered my sympathy and referred to the great loss to the community. I was encouraged when she said, "You will hear from us about support for the Foundation." Alas, that did not happen. It may be fair to say that what was happening here, Edward Johnson and the Board were waiting for each other.

Some months after this, Mannie Birnbaum phoned me to say Richard Tucker was in Guelph staying with Sid Brown who was prominent in the local Jewish community. "He wants to visit Edward Johnson's grave, can you join us?" Richard said he was on a mission of gratitude and wished to remember and pay homage to his great mentor at the Metropolitan Opera. We asked him if he would sing at the graveside and he responded with excerpts of several arias from operas beloved by Edward Johnson and himself. This became an indelible experience in my mind.

In the early sixties the planning throughout Canada for the 1967 centenary celebrations was in everyone's minds. John Fisher, otherwise known to radio audiences as Mr. Canada, had been named director of these celebrations on behalf of the federal government. I wrote to John asking him to speak to the Guelph Rotary Club on the suitability of a musical theme for Guelph's special centenary event. He phoned to say he was sending Nicholas Goldschmidt to speak to us on December 11, 1964. Goldschmidt was John Fisher's Chief of the Performing Arts Division. His persuasive personality was just what we needed when he proposed that Guelph had the potential to become a prominent centre for music in Canada. It was just what our fit of doldrums needed.

After his talk I invited Niki to my office to meet the directors of the Foundation. He told us he had in mind a proposal to hold the voice section of the annual musical competitions sponsored by Jeunesses Musicales of Montreal in Guelph in 1967. He said, "Give me time to work on this and I'll be back."

This was 1964, the year the University of Guelph was established. In 1965 Niki came back and I invited Murdo Mackinnon, Dean of Arts, Alex Ross, Head of English, and Ralph Kidd, Director of Music at the university, to meet with the Board of the Foundation, in my office. I remember how excited and relieved the Board was, especially Ed Crispin and Sam Luker who, with Mannie Birnbaum, Vice President, had been the most faithful Board members all through our financially strapped period. We arranged that I would step down and Murdo Mackinnon became

president. It soon became clear that Murdo and Niki knew the right buttons to press and they found a group of willing volunteers, on and off the Board, for the Foundation to sponsor The Guelph Spring Music Festival. As I write, the Festival has been a successful annual event for over a third of a century. Its early years depended a great deal on the knowledge and the easy but persistently persuasive ways of Murdo and Niki and their constant emphasis on quality.

A soft shoe performance by the first three presidents of the Edward Johnson Music Foundation during the 1983 Guelph Spring Festival.

22
MARRIAGE

The English poet P.B. Shelley (1792-1823) was responsible for this remark: "A system could not well have been devised more studiously hostile to human happiness than marriage". I want to refute that statement wholeheartedly since I have been fortunate enough to enjoy 4 blissful marriages, the last of which gives me pride and joy in my old age.

Earlier I mentioned how I met Gertrude Sorby. I was a no-show on arrangements for our first date. After that was reconciled we soon became the best of friends. Unlike earlier experiments with hot pursuits on my part, this one seemed far more sensible. My evenings up to 9 o'clock were used for studying but beyond that hour I was free to drop in and we told each other about ourselves or we walked and chatted if the winter temperature permitted. Gertrude was older and wiser than I was in exploring the elements that make for true friendship, before encouraging professions of love. This was taking place when I was a student and we both knew that I could not provide the financial security to justify a proposal of marriage. This was the prelude to a decision six months after I graduated, to pool our resources, and we got married on September 15, 1934. I was still using the legacy from my father to embark on a year of graduate study at McGill University.

Gertrude, my first wife (1935-76)

I mention all this because it gives me pleasure and I am grateful that we took a chance. We embarked on 42 years of marital harmony. Gertrude was pleased to return to Guelph when I began my career at the Veterinary College in 1935. Our vacations were taken on Caribbean freighter cruises which suited Gertrude better than the high social life on a regular ocean cruise. Her main problem was insomnia, which usually followed her to bed after hyperactivity in the evening.

Days of Leisure in Muskoka.

We enjoyed the Sorby family property on Isle of Skye, Muskoka. Her parents had been summer residents at Mortimer's Point since the turn of the century. We built a cottage of our own on the island as a centennial project in 1967 and it proved to be a haven, especially after my retirement in 1974.

Memories which want to compete with my present happiness in retirement include these Muskoka days and remembering our friends in Guelph. Our closest friends in Guelph were the Bain and Newbould families

Trevor's cottage in Muskoka, a place of peace and quiet. We called it Coediog.

and, in Toronto, the family of Harold and Hazel McDonald. There is no purpose in grading happy times but it is well to let them survive over the other kind. Good friends help in this. But tragedy visited us when Alex Bain died of a heart attack in 1953, leaving his wife Norma and 3 children, ages 2.1/2 to 6. Gertrude and I were godparents to these children and they took the place of the children we never had.

Gertrude suffered a protracted illness in the last 3 years of her life. She died in 1976. During this period she said to me, "When I pass on, you won't be lonely. I hope you'll marry Frances." Frances Barten lived in Toronto. She was a school friend of Norma Bain's when they both lived in Mount Forrest. Her lonely days as a widow found her enjoying her weekends with Norma. When Norma telephoned, inviting Gertrude and me to breakfast on several Sunday mornings, we knew Frances was her guest. The four of us had great enjoyment in each other's company and Gertrude's prediction began to seem likely. By August 20, 1977 our friendship got out of hand! I married Frances in the Chapel at Trinity College performed by her good friend, Rev. Derwyn Owen, whose father was born within 10 miles from Mold.

Frances liked to travel and we soon developed a pattern of annual trips to Great Britain, a fall visit to Radium Hot Springs and U.5. Ranch, and a winter stay in Victoria, B.C. for 4 to 6 weeks. I took her when I had discussions with the committees of Freedom from Hunger, in Kenya and Tanzania, for the Canadian Hunger Foundation, and she came with me to the Philippines for 2.1/2 months when I was a consultant for the World Bank at the University of Diliman, Manila.

I moved to live with Frances in Toronto after selling my house in Guelph. At that time I was Director of the Commonwealth Veterinary Interchange Fund. This took me to Guelph at least once a week and we stayed with Norma Bain overnight.

This funding program was financed by the Commonwealth Foundation and the Canadian International Development Agency. It operated for 10 years and I negotiated 160 short term visits for veterinarians who moved from one Commonwealth

Frances, my second wife (1977-1988)

country to another to learn a special technique in their research or to observe a program in the control of animal diseases which might apply in their own country.

Experts were sent to advise on teaching and research at veterinary colleges and research institutes in developing countries. This program had great interest for me in my early retirement.

Toronto proved to be a world class city for music, drama and other cultural offerings, and Frances and I indulged in all of this. Retirement for us had both satisfaction and enrichment beyond our expectations. Frances' longtime connection with Bishop Strachan School for Girls, teaching mathematics and physics, was ending but she still represented Trinity on the Governing Council of the University of Toronto.

It seemed that Frances and I had two of everything - she had a cottage on an island in Georgian Bay, I had one in Muskoka, we each had a car and a house, until I gave up mine. We made some changes in Frances' house and contents, building and furnishing a sun-room off the dining room, facing north, which made it habitable all summer, yet comfortable in winter. We practically lived in it. One of the three bedrooms was altered by extending the window area over the sun-room, making it suitable for house plants throughout the year. The garden became my pride and joy.

Princess Anne, President, British Save the Children Fund, on a visit to Save the Children – Canada.

Were we becoming hedonists? No, the serious side of life was also a busy part of our life. We both worked as volunteers for the Save the Children Fund, Frances was involved with the University, and I was on the Ontario Council of Health, the Board of St. Joseph's Hospital, Guelph, the Boards of the Ontario and Canadian Hospital Association. Yes, we had a very busy retirement.

This happy life was marred when Frances' doctor diagnosed breast cancer. She was very brave through her ordeal and the Sunnybrook Cancer Clinic told her she was their star patient. When she lacked the strength to be mobile she settled into a hospital bed in the sun-room and received the best of care by visiting nurses. Frances died in Sunnybrook Hospital on May 6, 1988. This brought to an end 11 years of a very happy marriage.

We had arranged to be in Victoria the following February and by that time I was ready for a change so I left winter weather in Ontario for early evidence of spring on the West Coast. We had stayed at the Royal Scot Inn every year for a decade at this time. A number of Guelph residents chose the Royal Scot; Alf and Mary Hales, Harold and Marjorie White, Ralph and Edith Kidd, and Alex and Mary McKay were among them.

I arrived in Victoria on February 1, 1989, having completed an examination to continue with a car licence the day before. The Whites had been at the Royal Scot for a couple of weeks before that and it was a comfort to have my good friends there to assuage the loneliness of being a widower.

On February 13 I was sitting high up in the gallery of the Royal Theatre enjoying the great music of the Sistine Chapel Choir. Just as the concert was to begin a lady sat next to me and we got into conversation. We had both left it late and could not get a better location. The lady said friends from Salt Spring Island, Dr. and Mrs. Liston, phoned her that day asking if they could stay the night with her - they were coming to Victoria for the concert. Her name was Elizabeth Quinlan. At the end of the concert she said, "I can let you off at the Royal Scot." I met the Listons and by the time I was due to get out, she asked if I would like to join them for a night cap so we went on to Pier One and we had a second highlight in one evening!

When Elizabeth saw me off at the elevator that night she said, "My daughter and I are leaving next Thursday for Rome to begin a European holiday and I think my car would be safer in your hands than in dead storage on this parkade." That began a firm friendship.

I had given serious thought to changing my residence from Toronto to Victoria and when Elizabeth and I were looking over the fence of a contractor next to Pier One I noticed a concrete floor being poured for a condominium at the harbour's edge. That, I thought, would be an ideal location for my new Pacific Coast home. We went to the office and examined the plans. I left a deposit and application to purchase the condominium that night and I've lived in it since March 20, 1990.

Shortly after I first met Elizabeth she asked if I would like to join a party of her friends on a harbour cruise on the old Princess Marguerite, with dancing and one-armed bandits providing a very pleasant evening. Most of her friends had moved from Edmonton to Victoria and many had shared happy times at their summer cottages on Pigeon Lake in Alberta. Elizabeth's first husband, Dr. Peter Quinlan, was an ENT specialist who had completed his medical training in Manchester. He died of a heart attack before Elizabeth came to live in Victoria. His colleagues, a gynaecologist, a radiologist, and another in general practice, had known each other in Manchester before choosing Edmonton as a new location for their practice. This move began in the fifties. The summer cottage friends also included 2 judges. I was delighted to garner friendships with such an interesting group of professional retirees and it all started on this harbour cruise.

Elizabeth had 7 children, one of whom died as a baby in Edmonton. After her last child was born her brisk preoccupation suffered a void! She filled this by completing a degree, Bachelor of Fine Arts, at the University of Alberta; the specialty she chose was to create things out of metal. She also took up the classical guitar, and joined a group who sang over the radio under the name of "Themselves". She cherished life and seemed to stop at nothing.

Alas, she was forced into a life of using less energy after she recovered from open-heart surgery. We were married in March 1990, when things had achieved a reasonable pace. However, on May 1, 1990 we were driving to Edson to visit Elizabeth's son Richard, and then on to Edmonton. I had driven that morning from Abbotsford to Kamloops when Elizabeth took over. It was her bad luck to have a puncture of

Elizabeth, my third wife (1990-1992)

the right front tire, forcing the wheel into a hole and turning the car completely over, landing right side up. I was bleeding from a gash in my scalp but Elizabeth was unconscious from a cranial blood clot. The clot was removed that night but she did not regain consciousness for six weeks, lying in the Kamloops hospital, until she was air-lifted to the Royal Jubilee Hospital in Victoria. During Elizabeth's slow recovery from this accident I could tell that personality changes were to be a burden from which she never recovered. She improved enough to be hospitalized in the Gorge Hospital where she had excellent care both in physio and psychotherapy but her head injuries remained a problem. On November 1, 1992, without any warning, she died of a heart attack.

It was with a heavy heart I tried to assuage my loneliness when Elizabeth died. To try something with a fresh start I decided to decorate the walls of the condominium to relieve the drab off-white lack of colour. A friend told me she had the right man for me. "He is a perfectionist as a consultant and practitioner in the art of interior decorating." Gary Sarian turned out to be just that. He came with a confusing number of wallpaper and paint samples but gave me help in his discovery of my preferences. I was delighted with the transformation and coziness of my home.

At Easter I took a bus cruise into the Okanagan Valley, ending up with three days at an excellent hotel in Kelowna. Here were a group of strangers, all happy with the outing, and I enjoyed their company. But it was a slow job yet helpful to try methods of escape from personal loss.

During my period of bereaving, Ivy Carlson, widow of a friend and a colleague from my days in Guelph, phoned up to say that the Victoria Hospice had formed a new walking group of which she was a member. Her husband had died the previous August. Ivy introduced me to about 16 who were in the group the following Saturday. We have all become firm friends, each of us sad about our own loss yet accepting the common bond that developed among us.

About two years after I had been with this group I was walking with Marjorie Styles one Saturday morning. She had just returned from Hawaii and I said, 'I've missed you." Her reply gave hope for my loneliness - "I thought a lot about you too." From then on Saturday morning was not the only day of the week for Marjorie and me to enjoy each other's company, with music and drama being helpful common interests. She had been retired for 8 years at this time. Her busy career was as manager for 20 years of Saba Brothers store in Victoria, featuring imported silk and wool fabrics and fine ladies wear.

Walking Group celebrates Christmas Party.

Walking Group have fun.

Marjorie lived alone in a house on Moss Street and enjoyed her lovely garden and huge pear tree. After about 12 months of this we found ourselves talking about "your place or mine" as an address for both of us. I wanted Marjorie to make the decision because I knew she loved 69 Moss Street, though I realized there were many pros and cons to be considered. Eventually the old house made the decision for us - the weeping tile around the footings ceased to weep and correcting this put it in good shape for sale.

Marjorie, my present wife (1995-)

On November 18, 1995 we were married at a family ceremony in my harbourside condo, which was followed by a party at 69 Moss, with all our friends helping us to celebrate.

Marjorie has given me great comfort in my advancing age and our mutually-felt love for each other is a delight to cherish each day of our happy marriage. As I approached my 90th birthday Marjorie would refer to the party she was planning. The event proved beyond my expectations. She sent printed invitations to all my family, including nephews and nieces in Britain, and cousins in different world regions. Fifty four guests attended, my nephew Ian Fleming, Professor of Chemistry at Cambridge University, having made the longest flight. My nephew Charles Law and his wife Lynn came from Barrie, Ontario; Jean McDonald and Jim Schroder, from Guelph. The rest came from Vancouver Island.

The walking group sang an ode to me and scatterings of verse, appropriate and otherwise, emerged from old and new friends, then numerous offshore messages with humour and best wishes, including an attractive hand-down-to-posterity certificate from the Prime Minster and a personal letter from the Governor General.

My good fortune is that I have been blessed in my old age with reasonably good health and more importantly having enjoyed four blissful marriages. When the first marriage came to an end I was 68 and retired when I ventured into my second. But the word ventured is used here only to point out the difference between the statistical average used in comparing the situation when older people find love and hope in a life-partner. I know my four adventures have helped me to live long and enjoy it.

My daily companions, now that I'm over ninety, are the words on the tip of my tongue that will not surface. In writing I frequently leave out the last letter of a word and omit the apostrophe, necessary to indicate the possessive case. These are minor items that are put right by proof reading everything I write. Among my new-found frailties the hardest to deal with is the names of people! I also tend to switch from my intention in carrying out tasks I set for myself. It gives me comfort to be told that this is the aging process, while the signs of Alzheimers disease arise from a different part of the brain. Keeping information on line is helped, I'm told, by the knowledge that comes from having had numerous and a variety of experiences. These can compensate for age-related memory problems.

But what has proved important to me is the pleasant ambience of where I live, the cultural events available, and best of all my friends and the constant comfort of a loving wife. I have indeed been well blessed.

Trevor and Marjorie dressed to represent Victoria's Seniors at a Canada Day celebration

Trevor inherited a new family when he married Marjorie.

Visitors to our patio.

Appendix One
THE BALLAD OF T. LLOYD JONES

The O.V.C. was 125 years old in 1987 and a musical evening was arranged in celebration of it. David Archibald, son of Prof. James Archibald, Head of the Clinical Studies Department, wrote the script for this event. He wrote this ballad, after looking at a 3 hour video when I was interviewed by the dean at that time, Dr. N. O. Nielsen. David accompanied me on the guitar. I had a standing ovation!

> A seed-merchant's son, I was nobody's fool
> Took a tea-taster's job back in old Liverpool
> My brothers were bankers, so bright and so keen
> They never suspected that I would be dean
>
> I toiled with my uncle all day on the farm
> Looked after the sheep and then mucked out the barn
> Then high on a hillside so fair and so green
> I'd read David Grayson, and so I would dream
>
> I'd dream of a ranch out in Canada's west
> I'd dream of adventures in contentedness
> Dream of the future and knew that one day
> I'd step on a steamship and so sail away
>
> I choked on the British Columbia dust
> My hands black as pitch and my eyes red as rust
> But someday a man must put stock in himself
> I packed my belongings and set out for Guelph
>
> Now, sometimes the world seems so vague and so vast
> And sometimes this life seems to go by so fast
> I arrived at the collge with my bags full of junk
> The world of a Welshman in one steamer trunk

Doctor MacIntosh taught us of cattle disease
And Fowler made castration look like a breeze
We learned meat inspection from old Henry Batt
And Schofield was trying ... let's leave it at that

The age of expansion was well underway
But Andy MacNabb was soon taken away
I stepped in to do the best job that I could
And hoped I could find a way out of the wood

I tried to recruit from the best in the world
And watched as the flag of the future unfurled
Blood, Jubb and Henderson started to write
And Downie and Archibald worked through the night

I hope I've not bored you with these little tales
The thoughts of a young lad just over from Wales
I think I have learned a fine lesson or two
And with your permission, I'll tell them to you

Scots, Welsh and English, they've all had a try
None of them thinking it pie in the sky
Aye, deans lose their souls in attempts to succeed
But now we're all happy that we've got a Swede

The years gather dust like the books on the shelf
And the *fondest* of all were the years spent at Guelph
Be true to yourself and receive what you give
So, here's to the college and long may she live

Appendix Two
HISTORICAL ESSAY[1]

As a rule people take little interest in matters that do not directly concern them. Yet nearly everyone in our western civilization eats meat. We all use the products of livestock such as milk and eggs as food. Much of our clothing - wool, furs and leather - is derived from animal sources. Medicinal substances such as cortisone which is used in the treatment of arthritis, insulin - the life-blood of the diabetic patient - and surgical gut come from various members of the animal kingdom.

Permit me to mention a few vital statistics. In Canada today there are over 15 million cattle, horses, sheep and swine and more than 56 million poultry. When our economy is compared with that of a country such as China, which lives primarily on plant products, it can easily be recognized that a high standard of living is enhanced by a well-developed livestock industry.

The development of hydroponics, or the growing of plants without soil, offers an alternative way of producing food. However, there is little indication at present that we shall change the nature of our fuel and become complete vegetarians. As long as man uses the products of animals as food and clothing, and as long as some parts of the world still depend on the animal itself as a means of transportation and beast of burden, the veterinarian will be needed to ensure a continuous supply and the high quality of these products as well as a healthy livestock population.

A report on the veterinary advances in Great Britain a few years ago stated that "the veterinary practitioner today is the physician of the farm and the guarantor of the nation's food supply." To put it another way,

---

1   This was my speech, delivered to the Royal Canadian Institute, in Convocation Hall, University of Toronto, in 1954. It has been revised slightly.

veterinary science involves the principles of medicine applied to agricultural production.

I am sure that the significance of the whole situation will become clearer if I remind you of the part animals have played throughout the ages in the life of man. Only by a study of history can advances be recognized. Veterinary medicine as an art is as old as the domestication of animals, but as a science is relatively new. It is known that the nomadic tribes in the dawn of history depended for their livelihood on the health of their flocks and herds, and doubtless attempts were made to preserve these animals from diseases through sacrifice to currently popular deities. No matter how cynical one may be with regard to the validity of the story of Noah and his animals in the Ark, one can readily believe that even in those times a far-seeing man would be aware of his dependence on animals and make attempts to save them in times of imminent peril.

During the long centuries in which tribes grew into nations, the fortunes of groups fluctuated according to the state of health of their livestock. Prosperity and power grew along with the acquisition of bountiful herds. Man developed complicated religious rites to protect himself from the numerous animal plagues which appeared regularly to leave a decimated livestock population in their wake, but gradually more scientific knowledge was gained as man learned how to preserve his animals in order to survive. Not long ago, an English veterinarian summed up this transition in this statement: "The veterinary art is somehow inseparably allied in its destiny with progress in human social evolution. It took several thousand years for man to realize that his happiness and ends were much better served by spreading the dung of an ox upon a field than by shedding its blood upon an altar."

The earliest veterinary literature, if such it can be called, appeared around 2000 B.C. An Egyptian papyrus dating back to this period has been found which bears prescriptions for remedies for use against certain ailments of dogs and oxen. These two species had been domesticated by the Egyptians for about 3000 years before that time.

A little later, preserved in cuneiform characters, the laws of the Assyrian king, Hammurabi, contain a well-defined system of veterinary jurisprudence. Here is one example: "If a doctor of oxen and asses has treated either an ox or an ass for a severe wound and cured it, the owner of the ox or ass shall give to the doctor one-sixth of a shekel of silver for his fee. If he has treated an ox or an ass for a severe wound and caused it to die, he shall give one-quarter of its price to the owner of the ox or ass".

Fortunately, nowadays veterinarians are not called upon by law to make restitution when their efforts are unsuccessful. And yet it appears that in those ancient times the doctor of animals was somewhat better off in this respect than a man who treated the illnesses of human beings, whose penalty was the loss of both hands if a patient belonging to the aristocratic class died after undergoing treatment.

Decrees protecting man against the dangers of animal diseases have been enforced since the time of Moses, who set up a system of meat inspection still practised by the Jewish people. In ensuing centuries, the Hebrews, the Carthaginians and notably the Greeks produced a considerable amount of veterinary literature. The great Hippocrates wrote on animal diseases 400 years before Christ, but he was in agreement with the Platonic doctrine that animals lacked souls and was disposed to deprecate studies in this field. The philosopher and physician Galen, who lived in the second century after Christ, was an early advocate of inspection of meat prior to its use for human consumption.

Apsyrtus, an army officer responsible for the maintenance of the Emperor Constantine's large cavalry force in the days of the Byzantine Empire, developed the veterinary art to a great extent. His descriptions of the diseases of horses, written about 350 A.D., are the best that had been recorded up to that time. Not only did he write on this subject but he gave instruction to his cavalrymen as well. Apsyrtus was the most notable writer of a group which flourished in the Byzantine Empire at that period. The writings of this group were brought together in a work on animal diseases entitled Hippiatrika. Historians tell us that the powers of observation and freedom from superstition exhibited in these writings were unprecedented. Osler wrote that, in contrast, the Byzantime period proved unproductive in human medicine, so that it can be said that at least during one era the veterinary art thrived independently of human medicine.

In the fifth century, the Roman, Vegetius, produced the first book exclusively on the subject of veterinary medicine. His contention that "knowledge is never mean nor contemptible and there can be no shame in practising a profession that saves the State from loss" indicates his enlightenment in an age when the writer on animal disease was considered on a par with the despised horse trader.

At this point, a short digression to discuss the origin of the term "veterinary" might be in order. The word is of Latin origin, and specialists in animal medicine of Rome were known variously as veterinarius, equarius medicus, medicus veterinarius. The profession was called hippiatry, from the Greek "hippos", or horse. A grammarian living early in the Christian era cites a verb from "vehere", meaning to draw, and defines the term "bestia veterinus" as "any animal that works with a yoke". Other students of language declare that the word "veterinary" is Celtic in origin, being a compound of two words, namely, "vieh", cattle, and "teeren", to be sick.

In the western European countries, practitioners of the veterinary art were called "marshals" during the Middle Ages, and later the term "farrier" came into use. In the English language the use of the word "veterinary" dates back only to the end of the 18th century. The French "veterinaire" was introduced into England probably about the time that a veterinary college was established in London by a Frenchman in 1791.

To return to our discussion of the evolution of veterinary art, from the time of Vegetius until the beginning of the Renaissance of the 12th century, any progress which had been made in accumulating useful theory in this field came to a halt. The barbarians destroyed much valuable literature. The Christian Church regarded animals as mere "brutes" and in general its dogmas were opposed to interest in alleviating the sufferings of members of the animal species. During the Middle Ages healers of animals were a despised and ostracized lot. Only in India where the lives of animals and man were equally sacred and in the countries overrun by the Arabs during their period of dominance in Europe was interest in veterinary medicine perpetuated. The Arabs are said to have valued their horses more than their women, and they recognized the importance of an animal industry to a prosperous empire. It was they who salvaged what knowledge of veterinary medicine had been accumulated thus far and kept it alive during the Dark Ages.

With the advent of the Renaissance, veterinary medicine began to emerge at the same time as human medicine. Men were making their way out of the tangled web of superstition concerning the treatment of disease and the very nature of disease itself. Guilds of men trained by apprenticeship in animal medicine were formed in Germany and England about the 14th century, but in later generations the treatment of animals became the duty of the very lowest classes. It has been said that before the founding of the veterinary schools at the close of the 18th century, "the most fortunate animals were those who escaped treatment, and animal plagues raged to about the same extent as (they would today) if the present corps of qualified veterinarians were banished from the country."

It was not until 1763 that the first veterinary college was established in Lyons, France, by Claude Bourgelat, horse master of the Academy of Equitation at Lyons and later inspector of the library in that city. Thus Louis XV, by whose order the school was set up, may be said to have sponsored the first institution of veterinary education in its modern form. During the next 40 years, veterinary colleges - 21 in number - were established in all leading European countries, including the first British school in London in 1791.

It is interesting to look for a moment at the situation as it existed in England prior to the establishment of the first veterinary school there. Education in human medicine was so poorly developed in England in the 18th century that it is not difficult to understand why so little interest was taken in diseases of animals. In that century, the veterinary work was in the hands of men of two different callings, and neither was remarkable for its erudition. The farrier, whose special interest was horses, was common enough in those days when equitation was of major importance. Somewhat beneath him in the "social" scale was the "cow leech" or "cattle doctor" who concerned himself with cattle and sheep. Such was the general disregard of these men that most of the people possessing any knowledge of medicine refused to debase themselves by studying or treating the diseases of beasts. To make matters worse, many pious souls still felt that animal plagues were evidence of Divine wrath and as such must be borne without complaint.

Unfortunate for veterinary education in England was the early death of Charles Vial de Saint-Bel, the man who founded the London Veterinary College. Thus the formative years of education in animal medicine in that country came to be directed by a human surgeon whose low regard for veterinary work was coupled with a desire to make money quickly by turning out large numbers of graduates in the shortest possible time. A young profession made up of men whose schooling in their field amounted to three months could hardly be expected to command much confidence in the public mind. Although this fault was corrected some years later, the picture was not improved by the existence of widespread quackery during the 19th century. It is estimated that in England in 1850 the qualified veterinarian was outnumbered three to one by the untrained practitioner. The average man at that period would still have agreed with the opinion expressed 60 years earlier by the editor of a book on cattle diseases, written by a London physician. Says the editor: "Cow doctors and farriers are in general the most illiterate, injudicious, and self-sufficient people we have amongst us … A wise man must think mankind in general either fools or mad who employ a set of fellows to prescribe medicine who cannot describe their properties, nor give a reason for anything they do … They injure the Faculty, discourage education and study, keep out better advice, trifle with the animal's life, and render the case incurable by prolonging the disease until it gets riveted in the constitution".

Yet the physician who wrote this same book formulated his own special panacea which he says has the following properties: "This medicine deserves the greatest encomium; it attenuates the pituitous sizy blood, dissolves its close contexture … detergeth the urinary piper … maturating the crude phlegm impacted in the lungs, dissolves … extravasated and coagulated blood … opens the pulmonic vessels … corroborates the parts that are hurt … obtunds the acrimonious particles of the blood … supports drooping spirits … drives out (the disease) from the centre to the circumference, turns out the disease, and bars the doors after it". I may add that Castile soap was one of the vital ingredients.

With the middle of the 19th century, we come to the migration of the profession to Canada. In 1860 the only veterinary surgeons practising in this country were a few men who had received their training in Great Britain. The instruction in veterinary subjects was confined to a few supplemental lectures given to agricultural students in Toronto. The political disturbances in the United States were followed by a great influx of settlers and a resultant increase in the livestock population and heightened interest in the welfare of these animals. The Upper Canada Board of Agriculture recognized the need for guidance in these matters and imported Andrew Smith, a young graduate of the veterinary college located in Edinburgh, Scotland, to found a school in Canada. Thus was veterinary education in this country given Scottish roots, which seems to be a mark of distinction in any branch of Canadian education and was ignored by such other breeds as the English, Irish or Welsh, to which select race I am fortunate enough to belong.

Professor Smith was granted a private charter and established the Ontario Veterinary College in Toronto in 1862. He was provided with no funds to aid this enterprise. The first class to take a regular course of study other than incidental lectures entered in 1864. This class, made up of three men, graduated in 1866 with the diploma of Veterinary Surgeon. It was succeeded by enlarged classes until almost 200 students were graduated annually by the latter part of the century, a fact of which we today are not particularly proud, for under Smith the College for many years had no definite entrance requirements and the course consisted of two sessions of approximately six months each. The school prospered, but most members of the profession who received their instruction there in those days were obviously not trained in a way which would gain the confidence of the public.

Yet it must be stated here that Andrew Smith was an outstanding teacher of the practical side of veterinary sciences. Several men, still living, who received their training under him, are revered by all who knew their work. James A. Campbell, curator of the Riverdale Zoo, was well known in Toronto. W.J.R. Fowler, who initiated the surgical course at the Ontario Veterinary College, proved himself to be one of the best instructors the college has ever had.

Educational standards were improved somewhat at the turn of the century. A marked advancement was made in the preparation of men for this vital calling when the Toronto college was acquired by the Province of Ontario in 1908. With substantial financial aid it was no longer necessary to induce students to attend by offering low entrance requirements and a short course. Since that time, the institution has operated under the direction of the Minister of Agriculture and was maintained by annual appropriations from the provincial legislature, until the establishment of the University of Guelph in 1964.

Under the principalship of the late C.D. McGilvray, the second big step was taken when complete affiliation of the college with the University of Toronto was effected in 1918, bringing the academic standards under the jurisdiction of the university's Senate. Since 1918 the entrance requirements have gradually been made more selective, the curriculum has been broadened and improved, and the course lengthened. In 1922 the college was moved to its present location in Guelph, Ontario, where it occupied the same campus as the Ontario Agricultural College, with which it became a founding college of the University of Guelph in 1964.

Before leaving the early days in Canadian veterinary history, I must pay tribute to a great name in Canadian medicine, Sir William Osler, and to his contemporary and friend, Duncan McEachran, a veterinarian. In 1866, McEachran, formerly associated with Andrew Smith, founded a veterinary college in Montreal. Soon afterwards, Osler, who was then associated with McGill University, began to take an interest in this new school. C.A. Mitchell, when director of the Animal Diseases Research Institute in Hull, Quebec, described the outlook of these two men in this way: "Osler understood and sympathized with McEachran's conception of veterinary education, and bent his great energies to assist. These two men were possessed of strikingly parallel views ... Each believed that medical science - human or comparative - is based on the same fundamental principles. Each believed that the fields of human and comparative medicine are complementary to each other ... that the veterinarian should be possessed of a sound general training, and that his position in the social order was not alone confined to the treatment of ill animals but had a wider and more important place. This was a radical view for those days".

Dr. Mitchell continues: "In 1876 McEachran urged Osler to set about the experimental study of a number of animal diseases. This was taken up with enthusiasm and during the years immediately following, papers reporting his original studies were published. These related to swine fever, verminous pneumonia of dogs (of which he discovered the cause - a parasite now known as Oslerus osleri), actinomycosis, tuberculosis, and trichinosis. Thus he was the pioneer investigator of animal disease in this country ...".

The Montreal veterinary school was absorbed into McGill University in 1889 - to be known as the Faculty of Comparative Medicine and Veterinary Science. The training given the veterinary student in this faculty was the best of its kind given anywhere in the English-speaking world at that time. It is a tragedy that within 13 years it was forced to close its doors, partly through lack of funds, and partly because its high standards could not stand up against the competition given by the Toronto school where a qualification could be obtained easily, inexpensively and quickly.

If I seem to dwell on the evolution of veterinary education please bear with me, as it is the field with which I have been exclusively associated for the past few years in my career. I wish in this connection to make mention of the late Andrew Leslie MacNabb, who was for 17 years the Director of the Division of Laboratories of the Ontario Department of Health, and subsequently my predecessor as Principal of the Ontario Veterinary College. In the seven years in which he held this office, the standards and facilities of the school were brought to their present high level.

In my day the aspiring veterinarian studied for five years at a college level before qualifying. When I discuss later the present-day scope of veterinary work you will understand why this was so. We tried to counteract the tendency to give a student a little knowledge of many subjects and comprehensive grasp of none. Entrants are required to have senior matriculation or its equivalent, as is the case in all leading educational institutions which prepare men and women for a profession.

Although due consideration is given to providing a student with an all-round general education, the basic sciences and pre-clinical subjects are stressed in the early years of the course. Anatomy, chemistry and biochemistry, physics, bacteriology and virology, histology, physiology, genetics, parasitology, pathology and pharmacology are emphasized during the first three years. In the fourth and fifth years, clinical work is emphasized, and special studies, both theoretical and practical, are made involving surgery, nutrition, public health and food hygiene, medicine and obstetrics. As in many other veterinary schools, we operate an ambulatory clinic which performs the work of a general practice, serving the neighbouring area. Through a rotation scheme in which students travel with this clinic, the final year class gains practical experience under the direction of two veterinarians who have been carefully selected for this work.

As in other professions, in Canada the right to practice veterinary medicine is within the jurisdiction of the 10 provincial veterinary associations. I am proud to say that the Ontario Veterinary Association has dealt very fairly with the graduates of foreign schools who have applied for membership since the influx of immigrants began in 1946. It will interest you to know that over five per cent of the present membership of the Ontario Veterinary Association is composed of veterinarians from Europe who have come to Canada in the past eight years. I can assure you that assessment of professional competence of these men has been fully considered. On this continent, most of the professions enjoy the right to run their own affairs and are supported by legislation giving them protection from encroachment by those who are not qualified. It must be recognized, however, that this protection must be in accordance with the axiom "the noblest motive is the public good". Reference to the absorption of properly trained immigrants into the veterinary profession can be cited as an advance in veterinary medicine, and offers a challenge to other professions whose selfish motives predominate over the public interest.

Like its counterparts in other medical fields, the function of a veterinary college is not confined to the training of young men who wish to qualify as practising veterinarians. There is an active programme of extension and research as well. The blending of these three - teaching, extension, and research - provides an opportunity to produce worthwhile results which would not be possible by dealing with one aspect alone. These three phases of our work are interdependent. The research work helps to provide valuable material for teaching and the stimulus required to spark the courses of instruction. The extension programme is the safety valve which insists that we be practical in our approach to the needs of the livestock industry. I regard the maintenance of a proper balance of these different programmes as one of my most important duties.

Let me give you one example of an extension service offered by a veterinary institution. An important disease which can affect cattle and render their milk unfit for human consumption is mastitis or infection of the udder. Thousands of samples of milk are sent each year to laboratories such as we maintain in Guelph, where they are tested for the presence of the various bacterial organisms which can cause this infection. Penicillin is used for the treatment of the commonest type of mastitis, but other antibiotics are also required, depending upon the species of germ causing infection. When necessary, the practitioner submitting the sample is given a report on the degree of sensitivity which the particular organism has for the antibiotic of choice so that our laboratory gives advice not only on the agent to be used but also on the amount necessary for treatment to be successful.

The diagnostic tests employed by veterinarians today, such as those tests used in ascertaining pregnancy in livestock, are based on somewhat more scientific principles than they were in 1688. In that year, an English farrier wrote, in his book which bore the imposing title, "The Compleat Jockey or the Most Exact Rules and Methods to be Observed for the Training up of Race-Horses": "To know whether your mare be with foal about Christmas, or no, pour a little water into her ear, and if she only shake her head, she is then with foal, but if she shake both head and body also, she is not with foal." Today we employ specific tests to detect certain hormones which are found in the blood or urine during the gestation period.

Most veterinary colleges maintain a hospital for the treatment of all types of animals, and the staff and equipment render a most useful service to the animal owners in Ontario. In the case of poultry and fur-bearing animals, as well as farm animals, diseases are diagnosed and treated, and changes in breeding, nutrition and management are advised where necessary.

Of special interest is our "proof of parentage testing service". When this service began in 1950 there were only four institutions on this continent where this work was being done and our laboratory was the only one in Canada. Unlike humans, no two cows (except identical twins) have the same blood type. A blood pattern as to type is inherited. Thus a valuable service can be given where a dispute arises over the parentage of a calf, when the owner registers the birth of an animal as required by the breed associations. If it is necessary to know which of two bulls is the sire of a calf, blood samples from the dam, the calf and the two bulls in question are tested. The pattern of blood factors present in each sample will reveal which of the bulls sired the calf by excluding the one showing factors not present in the other three animals tested.

This service was used recently to supply evidence which convicted a farmer of false registration of his animals. Suspicion arose when, in one year, 50 female calves and no males had been registered as being born in his herd. This figure is completely outside the law of averages. Samples of blood obtained by a veterinarian in the presence of two officers of the Royal Canadian Mounted Police were taken from one of these calves and from the animals said by the farmer to be its parents. The samples were sealed and signed by the Police and forwarded to us for testing. Our findings showed that the blood factors found in the calf could not have been inherited from these animals, and a conviction was made on this basis. This case established a precedent in North America since the courts had never previously accepted evidence provided by such a test.

In addition to services which require laboratory techniques, veterinary extension work includes consultation for veterinary practitioners. Veterinarians engaged in extension activities also participate in meetings of livestock owners for the discussion of animal diseases.

There is in operation a plan of veterinary services in the sparsely settled areas of Northern Ontario. This plan resulted from discussions at an Agricultural Commission of Enquiry held shortly after the end of World War II. Before 1945, only two veterinary surgeons were practising in these northern districts. Today, there are 11, practising under contract with financial assistance which provides each veterinarian with an income of an assured amount, half of which is collected by local municipalities and half given as a grant by the provincial Department of Agriculture. Fees are charged for all calls on the basis of a schedule which is part of the contract. The operation of this plan is one of the duties of the Provincial Veterinarian. It is gratifying to find that the owners of livestock in these areas appreciate this kind of service, which they knew little about until the plan was put into effect.

What are the prospects for graduates in veterinary medicine? There is a variety of fields into which they may go. About 60 percent of all veterinarians today are engaged in private practice. Very few are exclusively occupied with equine practice, which is due partly to farm mechanization and partly to the enhanced importance of food-producing animals and the rising reputation of Canadian livestock in foreign countries. In short, the emphasis is on cattle, sheep, swine, and poultry. A small percentage of practitioners establish themselves in urban areas and concentrate on the treatment of household pets. Pet practice is emerging as a primary choice.

The role of the veterinarian in public health is of paramount importance. His place in this field is due not only to his training in sanitary science but also the fact that animals serve as reservoirs of disease for man. The name "zoonoses" is given to the diseases of animals which fall into this category. The causative agent of some of these diseases is capable of infecting a wide variety of zoologically unrelated animals, while others are restricted to one or a few species. You can imagine, therefore, the importance of finding out more about the factors of resistance and susceptibility. Some disease-producing agents require a very restricted environment to live and flourish. If such conditions are available only in a certain part of the body of one species it will be apparent that the ability of the organism to set up housekeeping in other species will probably depend upon a slow adaptation to a change in environment.

An example of a disease that is restricted to one species of animal is hog cholera. An agent which attacks successfully a wide range of animal species including man is the virus of rabies - a disease that is occurring at present in Canada, particularly in wild animals and dogs. Rabies in humans usually occurs when bitten by a rabid dog. There was no evidence to suggest that the disease was transmitted among humans until 1947 when it was reported that homeless street urchins in Russia carried the virus in their saliva and human-to-human infection took place. Anthrax is another well-known disease that occurs in a number of animal species including man.

The public health aspect of infection by the organisms belonging to the genus Brucella, which I referred to previously, is interesting. Three different species of this genus produce a specific infection in the goat, the cow and the sow, causing abortion in each of these animals when the organism localizes in the udder and placenta. In humans, its presence in the general circulation causes the temperature to fluctuate, producing an undulatory type of fever. Infection from the goat is far more serious in humans than that contracted from the cow. Infection from the sow may establish itself in the udder of the cow without producing a clinically apparent disease, but when this is transmitted to humans it gives rise to a more serious infection than that originating in the cow itself. Brucella infection in humans is very serious in countries that rely on the goat for milk and meat. Since we in Canada rarely keep this animal, and because city people here drink only pasteurized milk, undulant fever is not as serious a problem in this country as it could be. There is evidence, however, that a great number of cases remain undiagnosed.

Records show that at least 80 infectious diseases of animals are potential threats to human health. The veterinarian is interested in advancing knowledge of these diseases, since traditionally he is responsible for protecting humans from the consumption of food that is not safe. It must be obvious that elimination of reservoirs of infection, whether in wild or domestic animals, is also a responsibility of the veterinarian.

To prepare the veterinary student for work in the public health field, he receives, during his undergraduate training, instruction in meat inspection, the production of a safe milk supply, and other aspects of public health as they apply to the field of veterinary medicine. He is given a basic knowledge of preventive medicine.

In recent years a number of public health units have been established in Ontario. These are organized on the basis of political subdivisions such as one or more counties. In his work with such a unit, the veterinarian finds himself one of a team with medical and dental officers, nurses, engineers and sanitary inspectors. In Canada, the teamwork necessary for the successful operation of these units began initially during a one-year period of postgraduate training at the School of Hygiene, University of Toronto. Representatives of the various professions just mentioned take this course together, and their close association gives them a better appreciation of each other's duties. The contribution of the School of Hygiene is providing this training in an environment of preventive medicine, and the broad scope of this programme are, in my opinion, too little known by the general public.

In veterinary science, the teaching and research fields are occupied by a few faithful souls who are willing to put up with salaries that represent less than half the monetary returns that are possible in private practice. As in other professions, their reward comes from the satisfaction and interest they find in their work.

Through the efforts of those engaged in the study of veterinary medicine, we on this continent have surmounted the first obstacle in animal disease control - that of the successful eradication of lethal epizootic diseases such as glanders and dourine. We are passing through what might be classed as the second phase - the eradication of the more chronic diseases such as bovine tuberculosis and contagious abortion or brucellosis which I have already mentioned. We now face the third phase - the problem of finding preventive and corrective measures for nutritional and metabolic disorders affecting our Canadian livestock.

At various periods in our history, some of the more serious infectious diseases could easily have been introduced into this country and become established here, had it not been for the vigilance of the government bodies set up to keep such diseases out. The country is free from bovine contagious pleuropneumonia and sheep pox which have had dire consequences in some other countries. The recent foot-and-mouth disease epidemic was quickly quelled. The serious horse plague, equine encephalomyelitis, has been kept to a minimum, which is fortunate as it is another disease transmissible to human beings.

I wish now to tell you about the veterinary services in Canada which were established for the purpose of controlling and eradicating contagious diseases of animals and to protect the public and the export trade. These services are organized as the Health of Animals Division of the Federal Department of Agriculture. The Division is administered by the Veterinary Director General.

The Contagious Diseases of Animals Act, a federal statute, provides the authority for the Veterinary Director General and his veterinary officers to deal with the serious communicable diseases of livestock by use of a "stamping out" policy. The outbreak of foot-and-mouth disease in Saskatchewan illustrated the effectiveness of such a policy. It was fortunate that the advocates of vaccination at that time were unable to influence those in charge to deviate from this stamping out principle. Vaccination might have saved the lives of some of the affected cattle, but it would also have permitted carriers of the dreaded virus to survive. In this way, foot-and-mouth disease would have become established in Canada and we would then have been committed to a continuous programme of vaccination which would be vastly more costly than the programme which placed all sources of the virus safely under six feet or more of Saskatchewan's fertile soil. It is recognized that we must maintain in Canada a livestock population that is completely susceptible to this lethal virus so that the disease can be quickly recognized and stamped out whenever it is brought into the country.

The control of bovine tuberculosis is an important function of the veterinarians attached to the Health of Animals Division. When dairy farmers at last realized the economic advantage in having tuberculosis-free herds, and that cattle with tuberculosis could endanger the health of humans, they supported the government's "test and slaughter" policy with enthusiasm. In Canada and the United States, bovine tuberculosis has been attacked vigorously and the fact that human infection with the bovine strain is now virtually non-existent is evidence of the success of the programmes that are carried out under government auspices.

It is fortunate that in Canada we have a centralized authority vested in the Veterinary Director General so that a uniform policy throughout the nation permits actions to be taken in an emergency when we are threatened with an outbreak of disease in animals. South of the border, state rights must be observed and federal veterinary officers must obtain the sanction of officials of the state before quarantine can be ordered or other similar action taken.

The Meat and Canned Foods Act is also within the jurisdiction of the Veterinary Director General. All meat and canned foods processed in establishments engaged in interprovincial or export trade are inspected by his veterinary officers.

An indication of the progress made in any science is the scope of its research projects and the possibility of immediate application of truths elucidated through these projects. The wide range of subjects involved indicates the investigational endeavour among veterinarians today.

Artificial insemination is widely used in the cattle breeding industry. Among the most important research projects in my day at Guelph was the low temperature preservation of bull semen for use in the artificial insemination procedure. This is the greatest step that has been made in the field of breeding hygiene since the method of insemination of animals was perfected. It may interest you to know that we have kept spermatozoa alive for 15 months and that we have proved the fertilizing power of sperm which has been stored for nine and one-half months. In the latter case the bull supplying the semen had been dead for nine months when conception was brought about.

The storage of semen for long periods was still in the experimental stage. The semen is mixed with glycerine and the temperature is gradually reduced to -79 degrees centigrade, at which temperature it is stored. Further research has shown how to handle semen in preparation for storage so that time is of no consequence and so that the beneficial influence of proven sires may be felt for many years after their death. Cattle breeders are already recognizing the advantage of being able to plan their programmes on the basis of blood lines proven by actual tests of performance of their offspring.

Of great help in the future would be a bank holding, say, 50,000 doses of semen during the time the female progeny of a certain blood line are proving themselves as milk producers. The bulls supplying this bank might die or be disposed of, but their semen could be used for many years after testing of their progeny had proved that they inherited desirable traits.

The long-term preservation of semen will also aid in the control of disease. Two important infectious diseases associated with cattle breeding are trichomoniasis and vibriosis. The former is caused by a protozoan which is killed in the freezing process. The latter is caused by a bacterium which survives freezing but which can be eliminated by the addition of antibiotics to the semen prior to freezing. It is therefore not too much to say that the storage of semen for use in the artificial insemination process will help to increase the efficiency of producing food of animal origin.

In our discussion of research work, mention should be made of the cooperation we have received from the Connaught Medical Research Laboratories at the University of Toronto. A joint committee formed by Connaught workers and our staff supervises a number of projects, most of which are related to the virus diseases of animals.

The Division of Animal Pathology of the federal Department of Agriculture is primarily engaged in animal diseases research. The headquarters of this Division are to be found at the Animal Diseases Research Institute at Hull, Quebec, and branch laboratories are located at Sackville, New Brunswick; Macdonald College, Ste. Anne de Bellevue, Quebec; Lethbridge, Alberta; and the University of British Columbia. Notable in the current programmes of this group are studies on atrophic rhinitis and erysipelas of swine, and Newcastle disease and pullorum disease of poultry. An extensive investigation into the fundamental aspects of immunology is also being made.

Members of the veterinary profession have made important contributions in the field of research. Let me mention a few examples. It was a Danish veterinarian named Bang who isolated the bovine strain of the Brucella organism, so that the syndrome in cattle is often called Bang's disease. Observations made in 1934 by Dr. Frank W. Schofield, head of the Department of Pathology at the Ontario Veterinary College, in connection with sweet clover poisoning of cattle, led to the present extensive use of the anticoagulant "coumarin" in various phases of medicine. Coumarin has proved to be of particular value in building up blood plasma banks which have played a great role in human medicine.

An outstanding contribution was made in 1893 by veterinary scientists in the United States Bureau of Animal Industry. Two Americans, Theobald Smith and F.L. Kilborne, discovered that the ravaging Texas fever of cattle was caused by a protozoan parasite which lived part of its life cycle in the cattle tick. Not only was this discovery of life-saving importance to the cattle industry of the southern states, but also the knowledge gained gave workers an insight into the cause and methods of transmission of many diseases of human beings including yellow fever, typhus, Rocky Mountain spotted fever, and malaria.

The extensive human suffering borne in some parts of the world by individuals infested with hookworms, particularly in tropical countries, has been alleviated by the administration of drugs which have been found by veterinarians to be effective against this type of worm in dogs - mainly carbon tetrachloride and later tetrachlorethylene.

The large part the veterinary parasitologist plays in the prevention of many animal diseases is too little known. A serious problem in many parts of Ontario is the large American liver fluke, a parasite which infests cattle and sheep. It has been found that this and other flukes which cause outbreaks of disease in animals and birds are most successfully dealt with by the destruction of snails which transmit the disease. We are currently engaged in ascertaining the species and distribution of such snails throughout the Province so that the disease can be checked at its source.

An interesting piece of work was accomplished by investigators at the New York State Veterinary College, which is part of Cornell University. Some years ago a disease occurred in cattle which was characterized by a thickening or keratinization of the outer portion of the skin. When this lesion was fully recognized, the disease, formerly known as "X" disease, was named hyperkeratosis. Affected portions of the skin are also rendered acutely susceptible to infection, particulary to the virus of warts. Because of this complication the early investigators were misled into thinking the cause to be an infectious agent. Certainly, a study of the lesions would justify that conclusion. However, one celebrated outbreak of the disease put the investigators on the right track when it was observed that the affected cows had consumed axle grease. This led the Cornell workers to consider the possibility of such grease being associated with other cases. Eventually it was found that chlorinated naphthalines, incorporated in grease used to lubricate the machines in processing certain feeds for cattle, were responsible. Later, the whole picture was made clearer when it was demonstrated that the chlorinated naphthalines destroyed vitamin A, the level of which in the blood of affected cattle was reduced practically to zero.

Various forms of cancer are common in animals. The benefits of research in this field will inevitably add to the ever-expanding store of knowledge of the fundamental process of tumour formation, and will no doubt be applicable to this serious problem which engages so many minds in the human medical field.

I have dwelt at length on the research work in veterinary science undertaken in the past and present on this continent. If time would permit, reference could be made to excellent work being done in many other countries, but I shall ask you to take my word for it that there is a universality of veterinary science.

The title of this presentation is "Advances in Veterinary Medicine" and yet I realize that much of my subject material has been designed to impress this distinguished audience with the importance of the veterinary profession to the welfare of mankind. The work of this profession is significant because of the serious economic effects occasioned by losses in livestock from disease, and because of the protection that humans need to prevent them from exposure to zoonoses. The confidence engendered by our methods of livestock disease control and supervision of food production and processing is of particular value in ensuring a market, at home and abroad, for Canadian livestock and animal products. I cannot emphasize too strongly the fact that we are dependent upon a thriving agriculture and that the veterinarian plays an important role in maintaining the health of this industry.

Perhaps we veterinarians have failed thus far to impress the world with the importance of our branch of applied science. It has been said that a physician having successfully removed the appendix of a man whose "scrap value" (if I may be permitted so flippant a term) might be $10, may collect a $100 fee for his services, whereas a veterinarian who has saved a cow worth $100 by removing a nail which is piercing its diaphragm and heart is often lucky if he can collect $10 for his services. The accomplishments of members of the veterinary profession have shown, I think, that they have the *know-how*; perhaps they just do not have the *savoir faire* with which to make their value known. They seem to have found it now as I write in my retirement. Have you required their services recently?

The institution of which I have the honour to be head has received excellent financial support from the Ontario government, but there are many parts of Canada where better support for veterinary work should be given. If present trends in population continue, and if we are to maintain the rate of consumption of animal products at its present level, each year it will be necessary to devise further ways and means of preventing animal disease and eliminating waste of animal products through improper methods of transit and storage.

I have made no mention of the social status of the veterinarian today. When I spoke to the University of Toronto Senate some time ago, I quoted an expert on social matters, and what is acceptable next door should be permitted here in Convocation Hall. The following is an excerpt from the newspaper column of Miss Dorothy Dix of November 3rd, 1936:

"Dear Miss Dix: We have decided to ask you to help us with our problem. My side of it is that I am in love with a young man who is studying to be a veterinarian. He has a nice voice, which he should cultivate. I am socially ambitious and I simply couldn't stand his being a veterinarian. Don't you think that if he loved me he would take up music as his career?

Jean

"I am the man and my side of it is that while I love Jean, I don't think it is fair of her to ask me to give up my profession. I have studied hard and I like it and can make a good living at it, while I never could be a professional singer. Which of us is right?

Willard

Answer

"You are, Willard. Jean is a silly goose. You would probably starve as a singer, while you will succeed as a veterinarian and if she only had sense enough to know it, veterinarians nowadays hold a high and respectable place in the social scale".

Dorothy Dix

GLOSSARY

Bosworth	A field near Sutton Cheney in England where King Richard III was killed in 1485
Bard	A poet
Brith Dir Mawr	Large home with mixed architecture
Barrio	Enclave or rural village in Asia
Cwm	Dingle or hollow
Creelman Hall	Dining Hall on Guelph campus
Cader Idris	Second highest mountain in Wales
Capel	Chapel
Druidic	Celtic priest (adjective)
Davis, Rhys	Welsh poet and author
Eisteddfod	Assembly of Welsh poets and musicians
Gorsedd	Ceremonial circle of stones (Druidic)
Gwernan	Place of Alders
Hemorrhagic Septicaemia	Infectious disease of ruminants, pigs and horses
Iberians	Early inhabitants of Spain and Portugal
Llyn Cader	Lake near Cader Idris
Maesgarmon	Garmon's Field
Macdonald Hall	Women's residence on Guelph campus
Parnassus	Greek mountain
Rinderpest	Virus disease of ruminants
Ricin	Poisonous protein in castor bean
Rickshaw or Jinrickshaw	Two wheeled carriage drawn by one or two men
Twll Tyfod	Sand pit
Tertium quid	An intermediate compound
Thorax	Chest
Tarn	Small mountain lake
Tal y Llyn	Head of the lake

Tot	Mug or large cup
Trans Humants	Livestock herders who move with the seasons
Squire	Chief landowner in the district
Sawspon Bach	Little saucepan (Welsh)
Westminster	British Seat of Government in London

THE AUTHOR

Trevor Lloyd Jones
D.V.M., M.Sc., LL.D.

A liason with a tea taster was Trevor's first experience in a job, but he could feel none of the nuances among different pure tea samples that were apparent to his boss. In any case, he soon found the bustle of Liverpool a very annoying contrast to the little town of Mold, his peaceful place of birth in North Wales. After three months of tea tasting he chose to move back. From 17 to 20 years of age he worked hard on his uncle's farm and he remembers the long cold winter evenings by the fire, with the opportunity of becoming an avid reader.

Now at 90, he writes about that period, enjoying the summer sun on his favourite Clwydian mountain above *Llangwyfan*, recalling with shimmering clarity a palpable vision which he refers to as his Welsh Parnassus. This was the beginning of Trevor's interest in the muses.

In 1929, on his 20th birthday, he found himself enjoying life at U.5 Ranch in the Columbia Valley of B.C., between the Rockies and Selkirk mountains. The following year brought this to an end, when he was kicked in the right shin playing soccer. A compound fracture of the tibia found him languishing in the hospital in Golden with time to consider his future. After crossing the continent in a battered car, he began his studies at the Ontario Veterinary College, Guelph, on October 1, 1930.

Graduating with the D.V.M. in 1934, he completed his M.Sc. at McGill University in 1935.

Dr. Jones became the first Provincial Animal Pathologist for Alberta in 1939 and, after a stint in the army on a secret project, he returned to his Edmonton Laboratory in 1945.

From 1952 to 1969 he was the Dean of Veterinary Medicine at the University of Guelph. It was in this period that his contribution to public service occurred. He has been President of the following organizations:

Save the Children - Canada, Edward Johnson Music Foundation, Guelph Little Theatre, the Rotary Club of Guelph, and the Ontario Veterinary Association. He was Chairman of the Board of the American Veterinary Medical Association. His experience also includes being a member of the Ontario Council of Health and of the Board of the following: Ontario and Canadian Hospital Associations, and Chairman of St. Joseph's Hospital, Guelph.

On his retirement from the University of Guelph in 1974 he became Executive Director of the Commonwealth Veterinary Interchange Fund (1974-1985), a granting program permitting vets in Commonwealth countries to travel and gain professional experience in other countries of the Commonwealth. During this time he was also involved in international development and travelled in several world regions as a consultant in veterinary education. This took him to India, Africa, South America, Afghanistan, The Phillipines, and Nicaragua.

Dr. Jones has received two honorary degrees: D.M.V. from the University of Montreal (1961) and LL.D. from the University of Prince Edward Island (1991). In 1962 he became an Honorary Associate of the Royal College of Veterinary Surgeons (London).

Trevor claims that his 90th birthday was a wake-up call to complete his memoirs. The book of his memoirs includes his childhood and farm experiences in Wales, his career in Veterinary Medicine, and commitment to public service. Finally, he touches on his extensive travel experiences.

ISBN 155212288-3